Jason S. Merrill

WILD PROGRESSION

Moonlight Grove Press

Moonlight Grove EDITION 2022
ISBN 978-0-578-28265-7 (hardback)
ISBN 979-8-218-03046-9 (paperback)
ISBN 978-0-578-28266-4 (e-book)

wild (adj.): lacking discipline or restraint.

progression (n.): the process of developing or moving gradually towards a more advanced state.

1

INTRODUCTION

My father grew up in a San Diego suburb called La Mesa with his two parents, a brother, and a sister. He got his sense of humor from his father and his intelligence from his mother. He was an eagle scout and was also a report to the nation scout for two years in a row. He won numerous awards in speech and debate in California. He was also the most interested in the LDS Church among the rest of his family. Many of them attended because of his positive influence. He was eventually called on a mission to the northeastern states, which at the time included much of New England and also Nova Scotia. He wrote home frequently and made his family laugh with his witty letters. Upon returning, he started attending college at UCSD and worked bagging groceries at a local supermarket. He then moved to Utah and started attending BYU, studying accounting.

At a fireside talk where Paul Dunn (a leader in the LDS Church at the time) was speaking, my father sat next to a young woman that was leafing through some sheet music. He tried to make some small talk and asked about the sheet music, but the young woman wasn't going to let him in that easily. She rebuffed his attempt at small talk, and he sat there in silence for a bit, trying to figure out where he went wrong. Then he got a different idea, leaned over and whispered to her, "Our speaker was also my mission president." That caught her attention and she started speaking with him more from that point. After a hike to the Y on the mountain behind BYU and an ice cream date over the course of a short amount of time, they decided they were right for each other. They were married in the LDS Salt Lake Temple and started their life together.

My mother was studying music at BYU, with an emphasis on piano, clarinet, and opera singing. My father never finished his bachelor's degree, but instead supported my mother in her ambition to become an opera star. She sang with the Seattle Opera Company, the San Diego Opera Company, and a prominent opera group in New York, while he did odd jobs to support them, including selling encyclopedias door to door. They tried for many years to have a child but weren't successful until after 8 years of marriage. I was born in Seattle in August 1978.

Around the same time of my birth, my father suffered from a ruptured aneurysm in his brain. It didn't immediately kill him, but it left him with severe brain damage. After the aneurysm ruptured, my mother and my father's brother-in-law had to teach him how to walk again and do other simple tasks that we take for granted every day. He was showing improvement in a variety of areas when he suddenly suffered a stroke in November 1980 and was hospitalized. While on his deathbed, he made a point of giving a priesthood blessing to any family member that came to visit him. It was also on his deathbed that he gave me a father's blessing. He passed away that same month. His family owned several burial plots in the El Camino cemetery north of San Diego, and he was interred there beneath an olive tree.

Some types of mental illness can lie dormant in a person for years and only become active if the person experiences extreme trauma. This was the case with my mother, as my father's death caused her to start demonstrating strong symptoms of both bipolar disorder and histrionic personality disorder. In addition to these diagnoses, she would frequently experience nervous breakdowns. These episodes would manifest in the form of extreme paranoia and pseudobulbar affect. In rare instances, these nervous breakdowns would include her threatening to kill me and herself. These episodes were of course very traumatic for me, especially when I was younger. The nervous breakdowns and the other general symptoms of her mental illness were negatively formative for me and ultimately led me firstly, to understand that my upbringing was not ideal and secondly, to seek for a better life. The journey that emerged from that understanding and desire, along with the unusual adventures I experienced along the way, are detailed in these pages and convey a story of resilience and perseverance.

I should make it clear that my intent in writing this memoir is not in the pursuit of fame or fortune. Rather, I have been told by countless people – friends, family, and acquaintances alike – that my story is too inspiring and compelling to not share broadly. I'm hoping that those that do take the time to read it will find it entertaining and thought-provoking. I also hope that it will motivate some, perhaps those that have the desire but for some reason or another have been delaying the start, to write their own story.

For the readers of this book that are less religious, I would take a moment to point out that not only do I consider myself a deeply religious person, but I also have had many experiences throughout my life, particularly during my mission, that were spiritual in nature. These spiritual experiences may be difficult for those without religion to internalize and believe. Nevertheless, with clear mind and conscience, I attest that they did indeed happen and remain very special to me.

2

HILLBILLY SASHIMI

My experience with small town living started with my maternal grandfather. As he got older, he started to suffer from arthritis. After some amount of research, he learned that the warm, dry climates of Arizona and New Mexico are ideal for those that suffer from arthritis, so he decided to move to Phoenix. After some time there, he discovered that he wasn't handling the extreme heat of the summers very well. In an effort to avoid this extreme heat but maintain the benefits of a warm, dry climate, he relocated to northern Arizona. About an hour and a half drive north of Phoenix is a small town by the name of Camp Verde (current population 11,000+), and that's where grandpa decided to settle down. Some people by nature choose to live their entire lives near their parents, and this was the case with most of my extended family on my mother's side. My mother and I were in and out of Camp Verde over the years, and one of my mother's brothers spent some time in Texas and Connecticut, but pretty much everybody else stayed in the Camp Verde area for over three generations.

When I was eight years old my mother and I were living in Salt Lake City, UT. My mother became pregnant out of wedlock with my sister, and in the mid-80's the LDS culture could be very judgmental of those choosing to have children outside of marriage. Not wanting to deal with this social stigma, my mother decided to retreat to the familiarity of Camp Verde and the somewhat less judgmental family she had there before she had the baby. Her father spent a considerable amount of time trying to convince her to get an abortion, but my mother was adamant about keeping the baby. My mother's experience with the baby's father was a one-time thing, so he was not in the picture with regards to our move and my mom's decision to keep the baby. All we knew about him was that he was Jamaican, and decades later mom decided to reveal his name to my sister and me.

My mom didn't have a job or a place to stay when she decided to move down to Camp Verde, which was typical considering her impulsive nature and poor decision-making skills. Just off General Cook Trail there is a small church called the First Assembly of God. A stone's throw north of the church building lay a dilapidated shack, the ruins of which remain there to this day. My mom made a deal with the pastor of the church that she would provide free organist and chorister duties for the congregation if he would let us live in the shack for free. He agreed and we moved into the hovel posthaste. My mom didn't have a car or a TV, and there weren't many residences near the church, so I spent most of my free time alone outside. I would roam the desert landscape surrounding the church, hunting scorpions, snakes, and Gila monsters. The shack itself was infested with large spiders, some of which we would kill, but not to the extent that we ever seemed to make a dent in their numbers.

One evening in July 1987, while I was on the porch enjoying the night air, I heard my mom cry out in pain and start panicking. I wasn't sure what was happening as I headed inside and saw her stumbling towards the phone. I could tell something was wrong as she quickly dialed a number. After she spoke with someone on the other end, she hung up the phone and turned to me. The time had come for her to have the baby, but she said something felt wrong compared to when she had me. Because of the complication and the proximity of the nearest hospital facility with suitable resources, they were coming to pick her up in a helicopter. Before long the helicopter arrived, landing in the desert terrain near the shack, and the people in the helicopter helped my mom into the chopper. Without any instruction or words of comfort, the helicopter took off without me, and I was left alone that night in the shack. Family picked me up the following day, and we all waited nervously until we received news that the baby was born and both mom and baby were in stable condition.

Eventually my mom was released from the hospital and returned to the shack with my new baby sister. She seemed so small and vulnerable compared to the rundown shack and surrounding desert environment. My mom and I both felt uncomfortable having her in the shack with all the spiders, scorpions, and other critters in the vicinity. One afternoon I was shirtless and barefoot on the porch, knocking rocks into the desert wilderness with a large stick in a baseball fashion. As I bent down to pick up the next rock, I noticed a medium-sized scorpion slowly making its way towards the open entrance to the shack. My newborn sister lay bundled on a chair not too far from the entrance, and my mother was distracted with something in a different room. I dropped the stick and the rock and froze, thinking quickly about what I should do. I perceived the scorpion to be a threat to my sister and quickly decided I had to do something to protect her. Rather than picking up the stick or finding something similar to squish the scorpion with, I started moving almost by instinct. Without thinking, I quickly approached the scorpion, raised a bare foot, and stomped on it as hard as I could. Luckily the scorpion didn't manage to sting me in the process, and after removing my foot, I could tell by the surrounding scorpion guts and lack of movement that it was down for the count. After describing my heroics to my mom, instead of receiving the accolades I was expecting, I got a massive scolding for being stupid enough to step on a scorpion barefoot. It wasn't too long after this experience that my mom started thinking it was time for us to find a place better than the shack, especially now that we had my baby sister with us.

My mother got a job as the music and band teacher at the local elementary school, which provided her with enough income for us to move into a slightly better area called Verde Lakes Estates. It was an expansive area near the outskirts of town that was littered with mobile homes and shanties that were one step up from the shack we left. The area also sported a creek and plenty of large trees, giving the residents a reprieve from the dry, desert atmosphere that characterized the rest of the town. My grandfather lived in a mobile home in the same area, and we started renting a very small home towards the southeastern corner of the community. With so many people now living close to us, I readily started making friends. One of the kids that I befriended was named Marty, and I quickly fell in with his crew and joined them in the poor life decisions they were making.

Marty had a unique home situation. He was 12 years old, and he lived in a mobile home with his 16-year-old sister, but there were no parents in the picture. His sister was nowhere near the troublemaker that Marty was, and she did her best to control some of his excessive behavior, but her efforts were not enough to really deter him. One time while we were in his backyard making a fire in his fire pit, he produced a pack of cigarettes and showed it to me with a wide-eyed look, as if he were eager to see my reaction to his possession. He pulled out a smoke, lit it, and started puffing, and then casually offered me one. I declined, and we continued poking at the fire. A few minutes later, his sister showed up, and Marty quickly threw the cigarette into the fire.

"You've been smoking again, haven't you!" she yelled loudly and abruptly.

"No I wasn't, I swear!" Marty replied.

"Don't lie to me, you little turd! I can smell it in the air, even though you're tryin' to cover it up with this little fire you got goin'!" she scolded.

Smoking cigarettes as it turned out was the one thing that she was unwilling to tolerate, which I found funny considering all the other things she let him get away with on a daily basis. We stamped out the fire and headed inside, on account of his sister ruining the mood outside. Marty started looking through a variety of VHS movies until he decided on one called Endgame. The movie was an obscure fantasy cult classic, with plenty of gory violence and even some female nudity, both of which I was not used to watching. I quickly became mesmerized by the film, while Marty stepped back into the kitchen area of the mobile home. I could hear him pouring us some drinks, while his sister made us some peanut butter and jelly sandwiches.

"Hey, leave that movie goin' and come back here for some sandwiches and drinks," he yelled over to me.

I peeled my eyes away from the TV screen and joined them in the kitchen. I took a bite of the peanut butter and jelly sandwich and then grabbed what looked like orange juice from a cup Marty passed me. I should have guessed there was a prank coming, considering the wide, goofy smile Marty had on his face as he passed me the drink. I noticed the weird look, but decided to take a drink anyways while I still had a mouthful of peanut butter and jelly sandwich in my mouth. As soon as I took a drink, I could tell it was orange juice all right, but there was something else added to it. Something very strong and sharp; a taste unfamiliar to me. The strength of the drink caused some sort of involuntary shock in my system. I felt a sneeze coming on, but I kept my mouth shut as I still had chewed up sandwich in my mouth. With full force, I ended up sneezing chewed up peanut butter and jelly sandwich through my nose onto the table where we sat. Marty and his sister both started laughing hysterically at my predicament, as I continued to be the only one not in on the joke.

"I spiked your orange juice with this vodka!" he proclaimed triumphantly, as he waved a small bottle of clear liquid in the air in front of me. His tone almost made it sound like he had some sort of cliché mischief bucket list that he was going through with me, and he was thoroughly enjoying every minute of it.

"Come on, let's leave, there's something I wanna show you," he said, after we cleaned up the mess I made.

"But we haven't finished the movie yet," I protested.

"Don't worry about that," he replied. "We can finish it up some other time."

We walked about a quarter mile away to a different mobile home, where a disheveled 16-year-old boy was hanging out on the porch.

"I got the money!" Marty yelled over to him.

"Shhhhh! Keep it down, kid!" the boy responded sternly. "Wait here," he said as he stood up and headed towards the thick brush and trees behind the mobile home. After several minutes, he reappeared and slowly walked towards us, looking down the road in both directions as he approached us. Then once he reached us, he fished a see-through plastic bag containing what looked like green leaves out of his jacket pocket and handed it to Marty, as Marty handed him some amount of money. We waited briefly while the boy counted the money. Once he finished, he looked off into the distance with a content look on his face, turned around, and headed back to the porch without a word. Marty and I took that as our cue that it was time for us to leave, and we headed back to Marty's house.

Once we got back to Marty's house, another one of his friends was there waiting for us. Marty put the movie back on for me, and then he went and grabbed a beer from his fridge. I had tried a drink of a Budweiser while my mom and I were visiting one of her friends that same year and thought it was thoroughly disgusting, so I made it clear to Marty that I didn't want any of his beer. He and his friend both started sharing it as I continued watching the movie. Once the movie and the beer were both done, Marty collected the empty beer can and turned to us both.

"Let's go, but don't tell my sister we're leavin'," he warned. "Be quiet about it."

The three of us headed down to the creek and found a nice secluded spot on the bank. Marty tossed the beer can on the ground, crushed the middle part of it with his foot, and then found a sharp stick nearby and started poking holes in the crushed beer can. I couldn't tell if he was making some sort of modern art, or if we were about to perform some sort of weird science experiment. He then pulled the plastic bag full of leaves out of his pocket.

"We're gonna smoke this!" he said in an excited tone.

"What is that? How are we gonna smoke it?" I asked.

"This is marijuana," he said in a quieter tone, drawing out the last word for dramatic effect.

Then instead of answering my second question, he carefully laid out the leaves on the part of the crushed can that had holes in it, lit them with a lighter, and then put his mouth on the opening of the can and started inhaling. Almost immediately he started coughing, and upon regaining his composure, said "Oh man, this is so good!"

He passed it to his other friend, who took a deep puff, coughed a bit as well, and then handed it to me. In spite of passing on the cigarette and the beer earlier, I decided to give this one a try for some reason. I inhaled deeply and passed it back to Marty. We continued like this for several minutes, and Marty was carrying on about how much of a buzz it was giving him, but I wasn't feeling it at all. As I grew older, I learned that when it comes to marijuana, the bud is more powerful than the leaves, and I also started wondering if the leaves the 16-year-old boy gave us were even marijuana leaves. If they were, then I had my first and last experience with marijuana at a very young age.

With a different set of friends, I would frequently go to the creek just to swim, hunt crawdads, and tire swing into the water. The younger kids would stay in the deeper area where the tire swing was, and the older teenage kids would hang out upstream where we could still see them. The teenagers would frequently bring beer with them, and the females would sometimes leave their tops and bras on the bank, creating quite the show for the boys young and old. On one such day, it was getting into the late afternoon, and the teenagers started building a fire on one of the banks. I was hunting crawdads while the teenagers drank and shared stories on the bank. After a while, I managed to catch a crawdad, and I brought it over to the group of teenagers to show off. One of the boys that was clearly drunk decided to have a little fun with me.

"Hey kid, did you know that you can eat crawdads raw? You don't even have to cook 'em!" he said drunkenly.

"Really?" I responded. I was extremely naïve at that age and remained so well into my adult years.

"Yeah! Tastes like chicken!" he responded. "Go ahead and pull those claws off so he doesn't pincer ya, and then pull the tail off, and you can eat that meat under his tail! Go on, now!"

I followed his instructions, pulled out a big chunk of raw crawdad flesh, popped it in my mouth, and started chewing. My first thought was, this definitely doesn't taste like chicken. As I continued chewing, the whole group of teenagers started laughing at me.

"Ah man, I can't believe he actually did it!" said one of them.

"Don't listen to him, kid, he's totally drunk and can't be trusted!" said another.

"Leave him alone, he's just a boy!" said one of the females in my defense.

I did finish eating it rather than endure the ridicule of spitting it out and looking weak in front of the teenagers.

At school I tended to focus my attention on little league baseball, soccer, kickball, marbles, and girls. Even at a young age, I would get into fights with other boys as we pursued the same girl, which would land us in the principal's office. Back then it was still acceptable for the principal to administer physical punishment in the form of a paddle swat to misbehaving kids. However, this particular principal had a very sizeable paddle, probably about an inch thick, wooden, very long, and including holes for what I presumed to be either aerodynamic reasons or to make the swat more painful, I couldn't tell which. I also continued showing academic aptitude at that age, winning the kindergarten through eighth grade spelling bee, even though I was only in the fifth grade and didn't prepare for the spelling bee at all.

Every Sunday the extended family in the Camp Verde area would meet at my uncle's house in the main part of town for a nice family dinner. Going there every Sunday became a highlight of the week for me. We had grandpa, my mom, my sister, and I, and then my uncle's family, including his wife, son, and daughter. His son was about 16 years old at the time, and his daughter was around 20. My 16-year-old cousin would teach me how to skateboard and kick a football around, while my

20-year-old cousin was more into card games, board games, and just talking. As it was with a lot of teenage boys in that town at that time, my male cousin was very much into dark, gothic type heavy metal music and culture. There was a band called Dio that he was particularly fond of and of which he had posters and art strewn across his walls. I've always been left footed, and he thought that was an abnormality, so he would always try to force me to kick the football with my right foot. His efforts were of course in vain and didn't cure me of my leftfootedness.

My grandfather was always very frugal. He had enough money to live in a proper home, but he chose to live in a mobile home to save money. Whenever I would visit him, he would remind me, "If you're going number 2 in the bathroom, you only need to use one square of toilet paper." I never quite figured out how to get the job done with only one square until he introduced me to what a bidet is. After trying it once, I definitely didn't want to try it again, so I continued to struggle using every square inch of that one square of toilet paper when the need arose.

His frugality was on display at fast food restaurants as well. On special occasions grandpa would take me to McDonald's for their Big

Breakfast. He would always get me a water to go with the meal, but one time I wanted a little something more.

"Grandpa, can I have some milk instead of water this time?" I asked him.

"Go over to the condiments counter there and get me a handful of coffee creamers," he responded.

I fetched the creamers and rushed back. Holding one of the creamers up in the air, he asked me, "Can you read what it says here on the creamer container?"

"Half and Half," I responded, which was the name of a free coffee creamer that McDonald's would offer in small containers at the time.

"Correct," he said. "So, using those math skills you're learning in school, how many Half and Half creamers does it take to make 2% milk?" he asked. "Four!" I proudly answered.

"That's right!" he responded with a smile, as he poured four creamers into my cup of water and started stirring. I started drinking it but didn't have the courage to tell him that it tasted nothing like milk.

As grandpa got older, my uncle decided it was time to put grandpa in a nursing home. Grandpa was always the self-sufficient type, so the thought of having staff take care of him in a nursing home was contrary to his nature. He was also always very handy. He was a watch and clock repairman by trade before retirement, and his mobile home was always full of the clicking, buzzing, and whirring of countless clocks on almost every flat surface. In his final act of handiness and ingenuity, grandpa decided he would rather die than move into the nursing home. He went to the hardware store and purchased some duct tape and several yards of flexible plastic duct. After returning home, he securely fastened one end of the duct to the gas source for the stove and the other end to a makeshift mask that he secured to his face. He then turned on the gas and returned to his bed, laid down, and waited for the end. As grandpa's heart stopped beating, his numerous clocks continued to tick and chime.

3

THE NATIVE AMERICAN RESERVATION

In northeastern Arizona lies the Navajo Nation, which is the largest Native American tribal land area in the United States. This reservation extends into the Four Corners region and spills over into both New Mexico and Utah. Within this expansive land area lies a much smaller Native American reservation for the Hopi tribe. One of several communities in this Hopi reservation is Keams Canyon, which as of the 2020 census had a population of 265 people. In the late 1980s, when I was in the fifth grade, my mother took a job in Keams Canyon as the music and band teacher for the elementary school. Keams Canyon is listed as a census-designated place (CDP) and is unincorporated.

I was one of only a few white kids in the entire school, with the rest of the students being of Native American heritage, as one might expect. I had a predominantly naïve and kind demeanor at the time and didn't know what to expect upon entering such a situation. However, a few bad apples in the student population made it clear from the very start that I wasn't welcome. Two boys in particular made it a habit to punch me in the testicles whenever they happened to walk by me, or if they found a chance to surprise me with it. The punches were never of the straight boxer jab type, but looked more like an underhanded pitch in a softball game. One time they even managed to surprise me in the boys' bathroom. I was standing at a urinal relieving myself, when one of them snuck up and punched me right in the jaw while I was still in the process. Not once did I try to hit them back or report their behavior to the principal, as I had the feeling that doing so would bring more antagonists out of the shadows and just make things worse.

I continued to exhibit precocious abilities, which my new teachers noticed quickly. Like many elementary schools, this one had what they called a 'gifted program', in which 6 to 8 of the smartest kids in the school would hang out for about an hour during the school day.

Because my mom moved us around so much over the years, I was able to experience a number of different 'gifted program' formats. This particular program chose to just make us solve logic puzzles for the entire hour, which was mentally challenging but also boring after a while.

I rode a school bus to and from the school, even though my mom worked there, due to scheduling differences. A number of the older kids in the elementary school would use the time on the bus to engage in inappropriate behaviors that they couldn't get away with on school grounds. Some of these behaviors were sexual in nature. Other kids seemed to have a desire to engage in drug-related behavior, but they didn't have access to any of the drugs they enjoyed talking about so much. In order to bridge this gap, one innovative young man decided he would try snorting powdered Kool-Aid, to see if it would cause any drug-related effects. I ended up trying it myself one day. It was definitely a painful experience that lacked any sort of hallucinatory effects. That didn't stop some of the older kids from pretending that they were experiencing exotic trip effects from snorting the fruity powder.

My sister was still a baby at the time, and my mother would frequently make me babysit on short notice if she had errands to run, or wanted to hang out with other adults. One afternoon while she was out and I was babysitting, my sister was taking a nap, so I decided it couldn't hurt if I left to go play in the nearby fields. I quietly left the apartment and headed towards my newfound freedom, without thinking much of the risk of my mother returning before I did. Once I eventually wandered home, to my surprise my mother was home already, and she went ballistic on me for abandoning my post. "Your sister could have been kidnapped while you were gone! What were you thinking?" she scolded. Without a good answer, I took the verbal beating and learned an important lesson that day.

When I wasn't stuck babysitting, my mother didn't care much where I was or what I was doing, so I was able to enjoy an unusual amount of freedom for my age. I made a Native American friend that lived not too far from our little apartment. We would spend a lot of time running around in the wilderness, climbing trees, throwing rocks at birds, and hiking the nearby mountains. The mesa tops of the mountains have a spiritual significance to the Hopi tribe. We would always feel a sense of peace and exhilaration upon reaching the mesa during any of our hikes.

One time while we were hiking in the mountains, I jumped down onto a large rock only to find out I was stuck. There was a gap between the rock I was standing on and the higher ledge I had jumped from, making it impossible to return the way I came. On the other sides of the rock I was on, it was too steep of a drop for me to jump down. I turned to my friend with panic in my voice and said, "I'm stuck here! I can't get back up there!" After trying to think of creative ways for me to get off the rock without dying, my friend responded, "I'm going to go get my dad to help you." I stood on the rock for what seemed like an eternity in the hot sun, waiting for help to arrive. My friend finally arrived with his dad, who looked down at me with a chuckle.

"Well, you've really got yourself in a situation now, haven't you?" he asked rhetorically. "You know, if I didn't help you and just left you there, you'd probably just die on that rock!"

I didn't find his humor amusing and instead just waited silently for him to get serious about helping me. He found solid footing and anchored himself, and then reached down with his slender yet strong arm to pull me up to safety. After that experience I tended to be more careful about having an exit strategy for any of my more aggressive bouldering activities.

When my friend and I weren't roaming the plains or the mountains, we would typically play at his house. He had World Wrestling Federation (WWF) rubber action figures that we would use to reenact the epic staged battles we'd see in WWF television programming. Other times we would sneak into the bathroom and look at his dad's nudie magazines. We could tell that his parents didn't have a great relationship, but we never talked much about it.

It still came as a surprise to me, though, when I caught my single mother making out with my friend's married dad one evening in our apartment. I had put my sister to bed and was playing quietly in my room that evening, while I waited for my mom to come home. I heard the door close and made my way from my bedroom to our living room. It was then that I saw them standing close together there in the living room, kissing each other enthusiastically. As I stood there frozen, it took them a few seconds before they noticed my presence.

"Oh, Jason!" my mom exclaimed in surprise. "I thought you were asleep!"

"Let me talk to him," my friend's dad said quietly to my mom, as if there were something he could say to logically explain their impropriety.

He gently brought me over to the couch and we sat down, while my mom stayed on the other side of the room. "Jason, your mom and I love each other very much. Sometimes when two people love each other, they might kiss each other to show their affection," he calmly explained.

"Yeah, but you're married," I quickly and firmly responded. I could tell from his facial expression that I had touched a nerve, but he promptly regained his composure.

"That's true, but my wife and I don't love each other anymore, so it's kind of a different situation," he responded.

I just sat there in silence. A few moments later, it became clear that my unexpected presence had ruined the mood for them. My mother said her goodbyes and sent him on his way. She then put me to bed, and I fell asleep with thoughts swirling in my mind.

Not too long after surprising my mom that evening, I started having feelings for a Native American girl in my class in school. Her name was Rhonda, and she was skinny and wore glasses. I would catch her looking at me from across the room during class, and she would frequently whisper with her girlfriend during class while looking at me with a smile. I was too young for any serious relationship, of course, but there was an intensity and a longing in the way she would look at me. Almost like a hunger for something she couldn't have. Perhaps I was a novelty to her since I was white. The way she would talk with me, it became apparent that her parents would not approve of me officially being her boyfriend. One time when we managed to find a moment of privacy, we held hands while gazing into each other's eyes, but it never progressed beyond that.

The occasion of any full moon had deep significance to the Hopi people. They even went so far as to name all the different full moons that occur throughout the year. Whenever there was a full moon, it was tradition in the Hopi community, for those that wanted to participate, to do what they called a 'full moon walk'. They would wait for it to be completely dark and for the full moon to be bright and visible. Then they would venture into the wilderness with family and friends with no source of light besides the moon. Some adults would even do the walk barefoot, but the desert brush wilderness was too harsh for my young, soft feet to attempt the barefoot approach. My mother chose to not participate in the full moon walks, but I wanted to be involved in the tradition. During my first full moon walk, I found the darkness and the sounds of the night to be quite unnerving. An elderly man nearby could sense that something was off with me.

"White boy, tell me what is wrong," he said warmly.

"I'm a little scared," I sheepishly admitted, as my friend and I stopped walking. The man stopped walking as well, while others continued slowly walking by us.

"Focus on that fear," he responded. "Feel it…try to understand it," he counseled.

I stood there in the moonlight, trying to follow his instructions. A coyote howled in the distance, renewing the fear I was experiencing.

The man continued, saying, "That coyote will not harm you. You are with friends, and you are safe. Let go of your fear."

It took me a few minutes after that before I started feeling the fear slowly dissipating. Then we were back in the flow of walking with the others. It was a special, almost spiritual, experience walking quietly in the dark wilderness with only moonlight to guide us.

4

THE ERRANCIES OF YOUTH

After I finished the 6th grade, we moved to an apartment complex in Phoenix's eastern valley, near Thomas Road and 48th Street. I started attending Orangewood elementary for the 7th grade. Our apartment complex was situated such that I had to walk through an unfenced cemetery each day to get to and from school. I quickly befriended a classmate, whom I will call Chuck for the sake of privacy. My apartment with my mom and sister was quite bare and indicative of how poor we were, so there wasn't much fun to be had at my place. Chuck and I quickly fell into a routine of heading to his house after school to play. Most of our time together was centered around video games, with an occasional R-rated movie sprinkled in, neither of which I had access to at my own place.

As our friendship progressed, we started to get bored with our video game habits and became increasingly focused on mischief and adventure. Even though I moved to a different part of the city in the middle of the 7th grade, Chuck and I stayed in touch through the end of high school and had many adventures together. The following events span that whole time frame and are not just limited to the 7th grade.

Chuck owned a couple of outdoor go-karts, and his home was adjacent to some open desert terrain, so we would frequently take the go-karts for a spin out in the desert wilderness. He also owned a pellet gun, so we would take turns shooting birds that were unlucky enough to land on nearby power lines. We were both fans of the Phoenix Suns NBA basketball team, so one day we decided to recreate the team's logo. The logo has historically been that of a basketball in motion with a sun directly behind it. We decided the best way to approximate it would be to set a basketball on fire and throw it high in the air. We tried coating the basketball in hair spray and then lighting it, but we couldn't get the flame to last long enough that way, so we decided to switch to gasoline.

I held the ball as he poured the gasoline on, and then he proceeded to light it. The flames burst so strongly that it frightened both of us, and in a panic I drop kicked the flaming ball high into the air. As this ball of flame traveled high into the air, I started thinking about all the dry, desert bushes surrounding us, and hoped the fireball we created would land in the dirt. As our eyes remained fixed on its trajectory, to our relief it landed in the dirt, bouncing around a little afterwards, but remaining far enough away from the bushes to not cause a fire. After the flames died out, without having any smartphones, cameras, or social media to capture the event, we simply turned to each other, smiled, and nodded in satisfaction. Mission accomplished.

After tiring of making and throwing water balloons at each other, we decided to start targeting cars driving by his home at night. The tall oleander bushes at the entrance to his property, coupled with limited street lighting in the vicinity, provided the perfect cover for us. We would try to time it, based on how quickly the cars seemed to be approaching, so that the water balloon would hit the windshield and catch the passengers by surprise. We would have plenty of misses, but that just made the successes all the sweeter. Passengers where we hit the mark would deal with the shock in different ways. Some would shout obscenities, while others would remain calm and simply turn on their windshield wipers. The best reactions were when they would slam on their brakes in shock, and depending on their speed, the screeching of their tires could last a while. Some would even slightly veer off the road while their brakes were locked and their tires were screeching, but we never caused an actual accident. It all seemed like fun and games, until one time just as we released the water balloon into oncoming traffic, we realized too late that it was a cop car approaching, and the water balloon was a direct hit on his windshield. We heard the familiar screeching of tires, but this time rather than eliciting feelings of excitement and accomplishment, we were instantly filled with dread. Our adrenaline kicked in, and we immediately started sprinting for his house, as we heard the cop throw his car into reverse to try to catch us. We burst into his house, deadbolted the door, and quickly turned off all the lights. His mother wasn't home, so it was up to us to just be quiet and stay hidden. We heard the cop car pull into the dirt driveway, and soon the cop was pounding loudly on the door. We stayed hidden, even as the cop started shining his powerful flashlight through the front window, in an attempt to find us hiding in the house. After a while he gave up and left.

Rather than scaring us straight, the victory gave us an increased appetite in antagonizing men in uniform. From there, on different occasions, we would go on to target multi-story apartment complexes and corporate properties that were fenced and staffed with security guards. Trespassing on these types of properties at nighttime became a regular, favorite pastime of ours, but we never crossed the line into vandalism. We would just find a way into the fenced property, try to find our way to the roof, if possible, make our presence known to the security guards, and then run like crazy to evade capture.

Our new addiction to adrenaline then led us into the world of tombstoning. We started finding and exploring the best spots for the activity across all the lakes, rivers, and waterfalls that the State of Arizona has to offer. We found a good spot for beginners at Saguaro Lake, northeast of the Phoenix metropolitan area. With a short hike, tombstoning enthusiasts can reach a point on the lake where there's a 20 ft cliff and a 40 ft cliff. The 20 ft one isn't too intimidating for beginners, but the 40 ft one is just high enough to strike a little bit of fear into the hearts of the inexperienced. The 40 ft one is also high enough to teach beginners that if you don't cross your arms on your chest and instead leave your arms out to the side, the water will punish you for it. On one occasion I brought my cousin to the spot and convinced him to go off the 40 ft cliff. However, I forgot to tell him to cross his arms. The undersides of his arms hit the water with such force that it let out a loud, sharp clapping sound when he hit the water, and he was left with severely bruised arms from the experience.

Throughout our adventures, Chuck's mom was a consistent enabler of our bad behavior. She would occasionally share her alcohol with us, show us her latest sex toys, and expound her amoral views of the world. She was a thrill seeker, just as we were, and was motivated by a constant search for fun, typically in ways that involved alcohol and sex. A social worker by occupation and a divorcee, she was involved in an affair with a middle-aged man, who was cheating on his wife. The man was a Dartmouth grad and a gym enthusiast. He didn't spend much time at all with Chuck and me but instead focused his time and energy on Chuck's mom. We learned quickly that if we heard Kenny G's sultry saxophone music emanating from her room, it was better for us to stay out in order to avoid seeing things we would rather not see. He eventually ended the affair and returned to his wife and family. After the affair was over, Chuck's mom's reaction to it was very telling regarding her character. She told us, "I told him that when he gets bored of his wife again, he should come back to me so that we can have some more fun!"

Chuck's mom had a likeminded female friend, whom I'll call Samantha for the purposes of this story, that would join her for various shenanigans. On one occasion, Chuck's mom and Samantha decided to go camping, and they decided they would bring Chuck and me along as well. I met Chuck and his mom at their house, and then we started heading over to pick up Samantha. Chuck's mom turned towards us in the back seat briefly while she was driving.

"Jason, you wanna see a picture of what Samantha looks like?" she asked with a mischievous smile on her face.

"Um…sure," I responded.

She handed a color 4" x 6" photo to me, and Chuck leaned over to take a look as well. To my surprise, the photo was of Chuck's mom and Samantha, both topless and in an oversized bubble bath, having some fun with the bubbles and each other. Samantha sported wavy, golden locks and maroon lipstick in the photo. The thought crossed my mind of who the photographer might be, and then I suddenly started feeling something stir deep within me. With a look of embarrassment and shock, I turned and looked Chuck directly in the eye, but I had no words in the moment. I nervously handed the photo back to Chuck's mom as my mind started racing with thoughts of what may lay in store for us teenage boys during this camping trip.

We picked up Samantha and her gear. As Chuck's mom introduced me to her, I avoided eye contact and felt awkward, knowing I had seen her naked before meeting her in person for the first time. Samantha had a bubbly, carefree, happy demeanor, just like Chuck's mom. We headed out and hit the road.

"So, where are we headed?" I asked after we had been driving for a while.

"We're going to a little place called the Verde River Hot Springs. There's a bit of a cross-creek hike to get to it, so we'll be camping a short distance away from the springs," she responded.

The thought of visiting a hot springs and playing in a creek sounded like a lot of fun. Arizona has several hot springs locations, but I had never been to this one. After driving for a few hours, we arrived at our camping spot. Instead of setting up our camp, we immediately headed towards the hot springs. For a decent portion of the hike to the hot springs, we waded and rock hopped down the creek towards our destination. We came upon a spot where the water was deeper and where a rope swing was attached to a tall tree on the bank. After swinging into the creek a few times, we continued on our journey. We eventually reached our destination and decided to all rest for a few minutes before heading into the hot springs. Then without a word, the ladies both stood up and completely disrobed right in front of us.

"What are you doing?" I asked in a panicky, confused tone, as they both casually dropped their underwear into the pile of clothes on the ground.

"The springs here are clothing optional," Samantha responded in a calm, casual tone, with a slight smile on her lips. Extending one hand, she asked, "Are you boys gonna join us?"

I was speechless for a few moments as I just stared at the naked women in front of me, so Chuck decided to break the awkward silence, "Mom, we'll have a look around and then decide if we're gonna stay here with you two or go play in the creek some more."

"Okay, boys! Suit yourselves!" Chuck's mom responded, as they gently stepped into a nearby hot spring. A fully nude middle-aged man appeared and joined them in the same hot spring, and the three of them started casually chatting. We started walking by them to check out the rest of the hot springs area, and my gaze inadvertently drifted down to the three naked people in the hot springs. The concept of strangers being naked in front of each other coupled with a complete lack of care was a new experience for me.

Once Chuck and I were out of earshot of his mom and Samantha, I turned to him and whisper-shouted, "There is no way that I'm taking my clothes off in front of your mom and Samantha!"

"Calm down, man," he responded. "I don't really want to either. Let's just go back down to the creek and hang out there. Then we can meet back up with them at the campground later."

After returning to the hot spring where Chuck's mom and Samantha were, we informed them of our plans and then left. We had fun rock hopping, wading, and rope swinging in the creek some more before returning to our camping area.

Our camp site consisted of a slab of concrete with a metal picnic table on it and a large canopy nearby to provide shade for our tent. I thought that Chuck and I would have our own tent, but as we set up camp it became clear that the four of us were all going to squeeze into the same cozy tent. After eating, setting up the tent, and getting the fire going, we all decided to take a break and enjoy the sunset and the fire. Chuck's mom had brought a plastic beverage container, one liter in size, full of a dark liquid. Without bothering to ask anyone what it was, I took a drink to quench my thirst. It predominantly tasted like Coke, but there was a sweetness and a kick to it that was unfamiliar to me. Without thinking much of it, I continued drinking it as we told jokes and stories around the campfire. That was the last memory I had of that evening before waking up the next morning. Feeling nauseous and disoriented, I woke up to find the other three already awake and quietly chatting. I stumbled out of the tent and headed towards the group.

"What happened last night?" I asked them in bewilderment.

"You drank my entire liter of rum and coke is what happened," Chuck's mom responded with a chuckle. "After we got tired of the fire, the three of us headed into the tent. You started running laps around the tent while we were in it, laughing and giggling as you went around. Then you jumped into the tent with us and started farting uncontrollably, while still laughing, until you fell asleep soon after."

I stood there mortified as Chuck's mom and Samantha shared a playful laugh after recounting the evening. They both assured me it was okay and that they weren't mad.

Our second adventure with Samantha took place just as I had joined the cross-country team at Brophy College Preparatory in Phoenix. I was a long-distance track runner for the first three years of high school, focusing on the half-mile, mile, and two-mile events. However, I decided to try the cross-country team as well. After practicing for only a week on the new team, Chuck called me at home one evening and invited me on a trip.

"My mom, Samantha, and I are going to Mexico for a week and a half, and we were hoping you could join us," he said.

"I just joined the cross-country team, so let me check with the coach if I can be gone for that long, and then I'll let you know," I responded.

After checking with the coach, he made it clear that if I was gone that long at that point in the season, that I wouldn't be welcome back on the team when I returned. I decided to choose Mexico instead of the cross-country team. I told the coach that I was quitting after only one week, and then later that evening I phoned Chuck to let him know that I'd be joining them for the trip to Mexico. The destination for this trip was Puerto Peñasco, popularly known as 'Rocky Point', at the northern tip of the Gulf of California. Rocky Point is only a 4-hour drive from the Phoenix area and is the closest beach experience for Maricopa County residents. Chuck, his mom, and Samantha rode in the cabin of the pickup truck, while I sat in the bed of the pickup truck without a seatbelt for the entire trip. The ride down went rather smoothly, except for a brief run in with the Mexican police. After crossing the border, we got near a Mexican town where it looked like the main road was partially shut down due to construction. However, the signage regarding the construction was weak, and we continued down the road. The Mexican police chased after us in their car and pulled us over.

In broken English, one of the two Mexican policemen said, "You can't drive on this road,"

"But this road is the only way to get to Rocky Point!" Chuck's mom protested.

However, the policeman just repeated his position. "This road is closed. You can't drive on this road. You all come back to jail with us, or you can give us $50 and we'll let you go."

Chuck's mom squinted her eyes as she started realizing what was happening. Having heard plenty of stories about what happens in Mexican jails, she had no intention of pursuing that option, so she paid the police and we went on our way.

Once we arrived at Rocky Point, we started unloading the truck at a shack on the beach where we were staying. We met up with a middle-aged American man that was half Native American and half Mexican. He had a very rough look but a carefree demeanor and was apparently the owner of the shack, which made us his guests. Over the coming days, we noted that he drank tequila and smoked marijuana for breakfast each morning, making me wonder how he was even still alive. As far as Chuck and I could tell, Chuck's mom, Samantha, and our host would spend most of the day just drinking, playing Uno, and occasionally going to the local marketplace to buy various items. Aside from our tequila-drinking host, Corona seemed to be the beer of choice everywhere we looked. It was so common that the vendors at the marketplace even accepted it as a form of currency. For one item I was looking at, the seller said, "That is either $20 or three Coronas." Craving a little more excitement than perpetual drinking and Uno-playing, Chuck and I decided to venture out away from the shack and leave the adults.

Our first stop was to the marketplace, where we had already been with the adults. We both purchased a large number of M-80 explosives, convincing ourselves that we would find a use for them once back in Arizona. M-80 explosives are illegal for children in America and require an ATF license for adult use, but that didn't deter us from our plans. We also both bought Mexican ponchos, which were in style in the mid-1990s with the cool kids in high school. We then started walking aimlessly even farther away from the shack and the marketplace. After a few minutes of walking, we heard the sounds of loud music and some sort of vehicle approaching us. We turned around and saw a Jeep approaching us and slowing down. The Jeep was full of American girls in bikinis, singing along to the music, all with a Corona in hand. "Get in! We'll give you a ride!" they shouted at us over the loud music. Having no idea where they were headed but a bit curious as to where the evening would take us, we jumped into the Jeep and the girls let out a cheer.

After about 5 to 10 more minutes of driving, we arrived at a very rough looking nightclub that was crawling with drunken American youth. I had never witnessed such a scene of debauchery as was laid out in front of us that evening. It was raw and lawless. Bikini-clad girls were staggering around with smiles, and couples were carousing on the beach. We headed into the nightclub, and it was there that I learned what a wet T-shirt contest is. Girls with bikini bottoms and only white t-shirts for tops stood towards the middle of the dance floor, while surrounding males poured out Coronas all over the females, drenching their white T-shirts to reveal their delights hidden beneath their shirts. Chuck and I just stood there and watched, declining the Coronas that were offered to us by strangers, as we just soaked in the madness that was unfolding all around us. We were both too shy to approach any of the drunk females surrounding us. As it got darker outside, we decided to head back to the shack so that the adults wouldn't start worrying about us.

Back in Arizona on a different occasion, Chuck and I decided to start experimenting with the M-80 explosives that we had bought in Mexico. We started by just lighting the fuse and then quickly throwing it away from us. Based on the size of the holes it was creating in the ground, we became convinced that if one of us were holding onto one when it went off, we would definitely lose a finger or two. Then, for no particular reason other than to increase the danger and damage, we decided to create some rudimentary bombs using the M-80s. We first gathered a bunch of empty, tall glass Coke bottles, which had an opening just large enough for the M-80s to fit. We would then light the M-80 fuse, drop it into the glass Coke bottle on the ground, and then quickly jump behind a protective wall. Luckily no cars or people were in the vicinity of our experiments, but we were excited by how powerfully dangerous the M-80/Coke bottle combination was, and how dead we would be if we didn't jump behind the wall before the glass shrapnel started flying.

This dangerous phase of my life came to an explosive end one Saturday during my senior year in high school. The crew we had consisted of Chuck and me, my high school girlfriend, and two male friends of Chuck's, one of which also brought his girlfriend, for a total of 4 boys and 2 girls. We started the Saturday with an early drive up to the Box Canyon Trail area of Arizona, which features some lovely, somewhat hidden waterfalls and some excellent tombstoning opportunities. As we hiked in the direction of the creek, we found gorgeous tombstoning spots that seemed to be increasing in height. Once we arrived at the first waterfall, we were careful to measure how big of a jump it was, but we were not careful at all in measuring the depth of the water. The first waterfall jump was about 85 feet.

"Any of you know how deep the water is down there?" Chuck asked the group.

"My brother has done this jump before, and he said it's fine," replied one of Chuck's friends.

That weak evidence seemed to satisfy all of us except for my girlfriend, who ended up being the only one to not do the jump. After we finished that jump, we continued hiking down the creek and arrived at the second waterfall of our hike. We measured this jump at 100 ft, and one by one those of us in the group started declining to do the jump, except for one of Chuck's friends. The rest of us started pleading with him not to do it, that it was too high and too risky, but he seemed determined to do the jump. He got into a brief argument with his girlfriend, as it seemed he was trying to impress her by doing the jump, as she tried to convince him it was stupid rather than impressive. In the end, he decided to do the jump, leaving the rest of us just looking on in disbelief and worry. He leapt off the cliff and started falling towards the water. When his feet hit the water, both his feet seemed to angle off to the sides, and his legs parted in a forceful and unnatural way. After he came to the surface of the water and swam to the bank, it became clear that he had injured both of his ankles during the impact with the water. We had to help him limp back to the car as we hiked back, but as the day went on, he recovered his ability to walk on his own.

After returning to the Phoenix area, we decided that we didn't want the party to end so quickly, so we decided to build a potato gun, which was a new experience for me. Some potato guns are built out of PVC plastic piping, but we opted to construct one out of galvanized metal piping. We bought a galvanized steel pipe about a yard in length, with an inner diameter of a typical potato, and with one end threaded so we could screw on a galvanized steel cap. This same all-purpose hardware store sold us the gunpowder we needed, in spite of the fact that we were all minors. We took all the equipment to Chuck's friend's backyard and started constructing the potato gun. We drilled a small hole in the end cap so that a lit match could be inserted to ignite the gunpowder. We shoved a potato down the pipe, put a measured amount of gunpowder on the inside of the cap near the hole we drilled, and then gently but tightly screwed on the cap. We lit a match and inserted it into the hole. We then heard a muffled explosion within the tube, followed by the potato launching far and high into the air. Success! After some high fives and cheering, Chuck's friend got an idea for the next potato.

"Let's triple the amount of gunpowder we put in there so that we can shoot it even farther this time!" he suggested.

After we all agreed this was a great idea, we put it into motion. We measured out three times the amount of gunpowder and again slowly but tightly screwed on the cap. Chuck's friend lit the match and barely inserted it before I heard the loudest explosion I've heard in my life, and then everything went dark.

The loudness of the explosion gave way to an intense ringing in my ears that allowed for no other sound to get through. The darkness in vision slowly gave way to a smoky haze in which nothing else was visible. As the ringing in my ears decreased in volume, I started hearing the sounds of coughing and female crying. As the smoky haze cleared and the coughing subsided, we started looking around, making sure everybody was okay. Fortunately, nobody was hurt. We started investigating what happened. The first thing we noticed was that the metal cap that was screwed onto the steel pipe was blown completely off, with the force of the exploding gunpowder shearing completely through the threads. We also noticed that a portion of a cinderblock wall between the backyard we were in and the neighbor's backyard was partially demolished. We came to the conclusion that the metal cap must have become a projectile, and that cinderblock wall was its first victim. We couldn't find the cap in the rubble of the wall, so we came to the conclusion that it must have ricocheted off the wall and headed in a second direction. After a brief search, we discovered a small amount of sheet rock dust and debris on an expensive car in the carport adjacent to the backyard. We looked up and sure enough saw the metal cap embedded in the roof of the carport.

"My dad's gonna kill me!" Chuck's friend exclaimed after seeing the sheet rock rubble on the vehicle.

We headed back to the area where we were operating the potato gun, and I looked at the demolished cinderblock wall once again. Then the thought came to my mind, with how forceful of a projectile the cap became, if the trajectory of the cap were any different, it could have embedded itself in one of our heads instead, killing one of us instantly. That thought was enough for me to decide, then and there, that it was perhaps time for me to put my excessively dangerous habits behind me for the time being.

5

THE GHETTO

During the middle of my 8th grade school year, we relocated from western Phoenix to a dilapidated area just south of downtown Phoenix. The catalyst for this move was my mother's worsening finances, which led to another eviction. Prior to the eviction, she had befriended a con man, who had lived with us for a short period of time in western Phoenix. I was walking with him to the corner store one time and got to see him in action, as he purposefully walked into a car that was turning right. He then proceeded to yell at the driver that he was going to sue him for hitting him with his car. He was constantly sharing his ideas with my mom on ways to rip people off to make a little money from time to time. He was quite the despicable character, but I was at an impressionable age and starving for attention from a father figure. He introduced me to the music of Pink Floyd and gave me my own copy of their 'Animals' album, which I enjoyed at the time. However, he eventually took advantage of us, and the financial impact of his actions led to our eviction. While we were at church one Sunday, he stole all my mother's money and valuables and disappeared, leaving only a short note behind saying he had left and wouldn't be returning.

After the eviction we moved to a neighborhood full of small ramshackle homes and homogeneous government project apartment buildings. We moved into one of the apartment buildings, the interior of which included linoleum flooring, painted brick walls, and an above average population of cockroaches. However, the rent was very low, and those responsible for doling out these units didn't mind that my mother had a string of evictions in her past.

To finish off the eighth grade I started attending Bethune Elementary, which was just a few blocks away. At the time (early 1990s), I was one of only two or three white kids in the entire school. The neighborhood consisted primarily of African Americans and included some Hispanics and Native Americans, but whites were very rare in the area. All of us in the area suffered from low-income situations, and gang-related activity was widespread. This was a time of government cheese, powdered milk, and powdered eggs for us. I made friends quickly at school and found the kids my age to be quite nice. I didn't experience any racism due to being white, like I did when I lived on the Native American reservation. I developed an appreciation for the music my friends liked, which led to a phase where I listened to nothing but rap. DJ Magic Mike, N.W.A., and Dr. Dre's inaugural 'The Chronic' were some favorites of the time.

Our neighbors were prostitutes that tended to work at night on the street corner just outside our apartment entrance. We didn't have a TV at the time, so sometimes for entertainment we would go out on our balcony around 9 or 10 at night and just watch the chaos unfold. One particular evening our neighbors were on the corner, and my mother yelled, "Stop doing that! Go back inside! We don't need that kind of thing around here!" It was at that point that I, her 8th grade son, had to explain the concept of prostitutes reporting to pimps, and how pimps didn't like business disruptions. After that discussion, she stopped harassing our prostitute neighbors while they were working.

One weekend while the sun was still out, my mother had some errands to run, so she left me in charge of my sister 9 years younger than me. Without much to do at home, I decided to take my sister to a nearby park and let her play in the sandbox while I shot some hoops. While playing basketball, I started hearing some very loud rap music that I could tell was being played outside at a distance. The volume of the music seemed to grow with time, as if the source of the music were getting closer to me. Then out of the corner of my eye, the source came into view: a group of about 8 African American men, all in their 20s or 30s and of various heights and sizes, one of which was carrying a rather large boombox on his shoulder, all of them casually walking down the middle of the street, and all of them wearing black pants or shorts along with signature deep blue t-shirts. The Crips.

My basketball dropped to the ground as I was paralyzed by fear, as my eyes quickly darted back and forth between my sister obliviously playing about 20 yards away and the group of gang members slowly approaching the park. In my mind I was trying to imagine a scenario where I ran to my sister and got out of there, but I knew they could catch me with ease. Before I knew it, the group of gangsters were slowly but surely walking in my exact direction. They got to the broken concrete basketball court, and one of them yelled out to me, "Hey white boy! Let's play!" After a moment of disbelief at what was happening, and realizing that perhaps my life wasn't in imminent danger, I started playing some pickup ball with them.

Even though I was only 13, I was already over 6 feet tall and had been playing street ball for a few years, so I was surprisingly able to enjoy my time playing with them. Some of them could dunk, which was well beyond my ability at that point. There was a tense moment when one of them went up for a shot and I blocked it hard, sending the ball flying. Everybody stopped momentarily and I briefly thought that I had just made a fatal error in life. However, the other men started laughing and ribbing the guy, saying, "White boy got you!" We continued playing for a while, and then I returned home with my sister without incident.

Through this and other experiences in the ghetto, I started to realize that I was not considered a target. That all changed one day in broad daylight as I was waiting for the city bus. Across the street were two African American men, each in their 20s or 30s, talking to each other while looking at me. One of them then checked for oncoming traffic, then brought his t-shirt up partially over his head to obscure his face and with a brisk walk across the street approached me. That day I remember feeling particularly down and was not in the mood to run or panic. Let the chips fall where they may, I thought to myself. In that moment I felt resolved to whatever fate was in store for me.

"Give me all your money, kid."

"What?" I nervously replied. Confusion set in for me, as I thought I was in for a beating, but it didn't cross my mind that this guy would think I had money worth stealing, just because I was white and on the wrong side of the tracks.

"You heard me, give me all your money or I'm gonna beat you down!"

Trying to think quickly on my feet, I slowly pulled my bus change out of my pocket. "This is all I have. I'm just taking the bus to visit a friend. You can have my bus money, but I'm just as poor as you." I turned and pointed in the direction of my apartment building, saying, "I live just down the street over there."

As he slowly realized I was telling the truth, he pulled his shirt back down and in a playful voice said, "Nah, man! I was just messin' with you! I wasn't actually gonna take your money!" He motioned to the other man across the street, who then crossed over to join us. "I didn't know you lived down here." The experience made for an awkward bus ride, as they both ended up getting on the same bus as me, and we all exchanged nervous looks at each other until they got off the bus.

My mom had an old Chevette that was in severe disrepair and rarely ran well, so I had to resort to public transit to visit my best friend in northern Phoenix. One week we made plans for me to go up to his place to help him and his dad with some of their remodeling. However, they said it was important that I get there early on Saturday morning. The public bus didn't run that early on Saturday mornings, so I figured out that in order to get to my friend's house on time, I'd have to leave around 4am and walk to the downtown Phoenix bus depot about three miles away, and then take the first bus available to my friend's house. I knew my mother wouldn't approve of me being out while it was still dark, so I didn't tell her about my plan. I set out and started walking in the dark towards downtown Phoenix. After about 10 minutes of walking, a policeman drove up next to me, lights flashing but no siren sounds, and rolled down his window. "Son, what in the WORLD are you doing out right now?" I told him my plan for making it to my friend's house so early, as he shook his head in disbelief. "You don't have any rocket launchers or hand grenades on you, do you?" he said in a comical voice. A weak attempt at police humor, I guessed. "Get in" he said, as he reached over and opened the passenger door in his vehicle. In spite of my great plan, he drove me straight home, woke up my mom, told her what I was trying to do, and told us both in a stern voice and with a look of sadness in his eyes, "You absolutely cannot be outside in this neighborhood at ANY time when the sun is not up."

While living in the government-subsidized housing, each tenant had a minor responsibility in maintaining the grounds. Our job was to occasionally water the patch of dry, discolored grass that barely passed as a lawn adjacent to the southern wall of our unit. Our unit was upstairs and accessible via a concrete and steel staircase on the south side of the same building. We would typically accomplish this task by turning the sprinkler water on once it had cooled down for the day, and then turning the water off before turning in for the night. One evening, while my mom and I were on the balcony enjoying the mischief unfolding before our eyes, my ears picked up the sound of running water.

"Mom, I left the water on down there by accident. I need to go down there really quick and turn it off," I told her.

With a look of pure terror in her eyes, she exclaimed, "Jason! You can't go out there at this time of night! It's too dangerous!"

"I'll be fine," I said. "It's just near the bottom of the stairs, and then I'll come right back in."

"No! Please just leave the water running overnight and we can handle it in the morning," she replied.

Not wanting her to get in trouble for leaving the water running all night, I ignored her plea and headed out the door. To my surprise, as soon as I cleared the entrance, I heard her quickly close the door behind me and lock the deadbolt. Not quite sure how to process her locking the door for what I thought would be such a brief period of time, I headed down the stairs.

The sprinkler water valve was on the southern wall of our unit. As I kneeled down to turn it off, my peripheral vision picked up a pack of kids running east from behind the apartment complex across the street just south of our unit. It wasn't unusual to see kids out that late, as there were plenty of parents that were not as responsible as my mom in keeping younger children inside at night. However, as I turned my head to get a better look at the pack of kids running away from something or someone I couldn't see behind that apartment complex, my eyes picked up something new. Between the complex just to the south of us across the street, and the complex directly west of that one, stood an adult in some sort of a trenchcoat, holding a handgun in his right hand in a palm down fashion, pointing it towards something or someone I couldn't see in the vicinity of where the kids had been before they started running. Seeing the raised gun paralyzed me with fear, and then I heard a handful of shots ring out, with no returning gunfire. The figure in the trenchcoat then ran towards the north side of the complex southwest of ours and across the street, and he then bounded up the stairs and into one of the apartment units. I quickly finished turning off the water and then ran up our own set of stairs, and proceeded to bang on the door, yelling to my mom that it was me, trying to shake her from the daze I'm sure she was experiencing from hearing gunshots within such a close range while her son was still outside. After taking a verbal beating from her for defying her wishes, we slowly returned to the balcony, both of us still too shaken up to go to bed, and also curious to see what would happen next after the shooting we just witnessed. Slowly but surely, marked and unmarked police vehicles started filing into our small street. After a dramatic forced entry at the unit where the shooter had retreated to, the police started lining up potential perpetrators on the curb just outside that apartment unit. We learned the next day that the shooting had led to one of the biggest drug busts the Phoenix police had ever completed, right across the street from us.

After finishing the 8th grade at Bethune Elementary, the time came for me to choose a high school to attend. There were two public high schools that we could choose from: South Mountain High School or Central High School. At the time, both high schools were known for having trouble with weapons, drugs, and gang activity. Before moving to the ghetto, I had attended Royal Palm junior high and had befriended a number boys from very wealthy homes. I had recalled them talking about their intent to go to a place called Brophy for high school. Not fully understanding the implications or requirements of attending an all-boys private Jesuit catholic high school, part of me wished I could escape the prospects of attending South Mountain or Central. When my mom asked me which high school I wanted to attend, I replied, "I want to go to Brophy!" with a tone of naïve excitedness.

Never one to back down from big moves in life, my mother loaded up me and my sister in her jalopy and drove us to Brophy. After a period of looking around, we finally found the main administration office, which was luckily staffed at the time. We walked in, and my mother commenced her magic. "My son wants to go here. We're really poor and can't afford the tuition, but he's really smart." After the initial wide-eyed shock wore off of the ladies' faces in the room, one of them said, "Well, we have an entrance exam. Let's take him into another room and we'll see how he does." After seeing the results of my exam, they offered me a full-ride scholarship. Thanks to their generosity, I was able to attend Brophy without ever paying a dime. They did have me do some odd jobs over the years, including dishes at the priests' residence, manning the school switchboard, classroom janitorial work, and serving as waitstaff for occasional classy donor dinners. However, I was happy to do these odd jobs, knowing that I was getting a much better education than I would have if I went to one of the public high schools near our apartment.

Eventually we escaped the ghetto, but I'll always remember the words of one of my African American friends during my time in that area. We were on his balcony, lifting makeshift weights made by filling empty milk gallon containers with dirt, since we were both too poor to afford real weights. As we sat there lifting weights, he suddenly paused, looked vaguely into the distance and said, "Man, I wanna leave this place, but I feel like I'm stuck here."

6

LEAVING HOME EARLY

A defining characteristic of my childhood was our constant moving from apartment to apartment, resulting from a combination of my mother's impulsive nature and frequent evictions due to unpaid rent. Before high school I never attended the same school for more than a year. Moving so frequently led to a string of disappointments with my childhood friendships – as soon as I made new friends, we would move again. Since I was young and this lifestyle was all I knew, I didn't realize how unusual it was that we would move so frequently, and I wasn't in the habit of protesting much whenever my mom decided it was time to pick up and move. I was always disappointed about each move, but I didn't have any power in the situation and was never successful in changing my mother's mind once she had decided to move.

This all changed when I reached my pre-teen years. In the 6th and 7th grades I met my two childhood best friends at different schools, and I didn't want to lose their friendship even though we continued to move around the Phoenix valley. To make these friendships continue, I would take the city bus to visit them at their homes, or to meet up somewhere else for various activities. I got quite good at hopping on the city bus by myself to get around and travel several miles away from home, even at the young age of 12. Most parents wouldn't give their children that level of freedom at such an early age, but from a young age my mom had pretty much let me come and go as I please. I enjoyed the freedom, but I couldn't help feeling that there was an aspect of neglect in there as well with regards to how my mom cared for me and my sister.

These newfound city bus skills started coming in handy once I started attending Brophy College Preparatory. I felt that I had been given a tremendous gift by being accepted there on scholarship, and I didn't want my mother's continuous moves to interrupt my education there. Instead of switching schools every time we moved, like I did in my elementary school years, I started taking city transit to continue my high school education at Brophy, even as my mother continued to move around the Phoenix valley. This approach seemed to work well, until the middle of my junior year when everything started falling apart.

Towards the end of the first semester of my junior year, I came home from school to find my mom in a distraught but determined mood. The prior week we had been in a fight, because she chose to pay the phone bill instead of the rent, and now we were getting evicted again. They also turned off our electricity because she failed to pay the electric bill. "Jason, I've decided we're going to move back to Camp Verde. You can drop out of Brophy – just quit high school altogether, and get a job to help support the family once we get up there." The prospect of losing everything I had worked towards with my private high school education weighed heavily on my mind. My mom was sick at the time, so she had me do the vast majority of the packing for the new move. That evening as I was studying flashcards by candlelight for one of my upcoming midterm exams, I was suddenly struck by how ridiculous the whole situation was. In that candlelit moment, I made a big decision without thinking about the consequences. I put my flashcards away, grabbed the candle, and walked into my mom's room. "I'm not going with you," I said calmly. Her initial look of surprise gave way to a resolute demeanor as she simply responded, "Well, I'm still going!" I walked back to my room, blew out the candle, and went to sleep.

The next morning I left for school with just my backpack and no further discussion with my mother. I was determined to not come back home after school that day, but I had no feasible way of bringing any belongings with me, other than what I could fit in my backpack. After finishing the day's classes, I ventured over to the office of Brophy's president, who also happened to be a catholic priest. I relayed my situation to him, and he said, "I'm going to need a few days, but let me see what I can do." Not knowing where I was going to sleep that night, I decided to call my best friend from one of the school phones. I told him the whole story and asked if I could crash at his place while I figured out where I was going to go. He spoke with his mom about it briefly and then returned to our call:

"We're actually headed out right now for a family vacation up to Alaska, but my mom says you can housesit for us while we're gone. We'll be back after the new year, and you'll have to find a different place to stay before we get back."

I could tell by his response that his mom didn't want to end up with another kid in her house, but I was grateful that I at least had a bed and a roof over my head until I could figure out my next move.

I finished off the semester's classes and midterm exams before the holiday break over the next few days, and then I returned to the president's office to see if he had made any progress in helping me find a new housing arrangement. To my surprise he had found something, and things started looking up.

"There is a boys' home right next to the baseball field, and they have agreed to take you in," he said. "Usually there is an application and vetting process before a boy can enter the home, but I was able to expedite all of that to get you in there as soon as possible. Unfortunately, you won't be able to move in until the first week of January, so you'll need to maintain your temporary housing until then."

I went to my friend's house that evening happy, knowing that I'd have a new place to stay long-term. The next couple weeks were heart-wrenching. At 16, I was essentially homeless and spending Christmas alone. I felt alone in the world, with an unfair burden on my shoulders. Soon the new year came, life felt a little brighter, and I moved into the boys' home spot the school had arranged for me: the Phoenix branch of the international Boys Hope Girls Hope organization.

Life in the boys' home was a big adjustment from what I had become accustomed to in my childhood. Freedoms that I had enjoyed for years were now restricted, which is to say that they were now age-appropriate. The staff were very caring people, and for the first time in my life, my living situation was stable. I was now free to focus on my schoolwork without worrying about when the next eviction would come, or if we'd have electricity when I returned home from school. This emotional stability helped me perform better in school and helped me become a generally happier person. I quickly settled into the rhythm and structure they had for the boys. Daily chores, scheduled time for studying and homework, some free time, snack time, lights out, and bed time. Some of the boys in the home came from very rough backgrounds, but we all respected the structure of the home and did our best to comply with the staff's requests.

This was the mid 90's, before smartphones had taken over everybody's lives. To entertain ourselves we would play Mortal Kombat on the Sega Genesis, we would play billiards, we would read books, listen to music CDs, play chess, play basketball, play Magic the Gathering (a collectible card game), and lift weights. Those of us that struggled less with school would also typically help tutor the boys that might be struggling. We had a TV in the home, but we rarely watched any TV shows or movies on it. The boys had a shared computer in the loft, an old Apple IIe that we used primarily for word processing for various high school assignments. All of the other boys in the home were either Hispanic or Native American, and we all came from very different family situations, but we all pretty much got along as brothers.

Not long after I entered the boys' home, I also started my relationship with my high school girlfriend. We had actually met at Royal Palm junior high a few years prior, where I was Romeo and she was Juliet in the school play. In junior high I was more interested in basketball and video games, while she was frustrated that I wouldn't actually make contact with her when I pretended to kiss her in the school play. She ended up attending the same public high school, Sunnyslope High, as my best friend in northern Phoenix. They ended up doing a physics project together and were working on the project in his room when she noticed a picture of my best friend and me together. My friend later relayed to me how the conversation went:

"You know Jason Merrill?" she asked.

"Know him?" he responded. "We've been best friends since the 6th grade."

"Here's my number," she replied. "Tell him to call me."

Mustering the courage to call her brought butterflies to my stomach, but our initial conversation was magical. She lived miles away from the boys' home, but she had a car and was willing to pick me up for dates. Her friendship throughout the rest of my high school experience was a source of comfort and strength to me when times got rough in the boys' home. It didn't work out for our relationship to continue once I left Arizona for college, but I have fond memories of the good times we had over the course of our relationship.

The Boys Hope Girls Hope organization was founded by a catholic priest, which was an important part of the organization's heritage. However, the organization also recognized that the boys that entered the home came from diverse religious backgrounds. As such the organization was set up to require some sort of participation in organized religion, but the boys were free to participate in services other than catholic mass. The religious participation requirement was a smart one in my view, as some of the boys came from backgrounds where they may have received questionable moral upbringing. Mandatory church attendance was one way for the organization to get the boys back up to speed with regards to general moral decision making. The spiritual requirement ended up throwing me into a period of self-reflection, as I struggled to reconcile my religious background with my newfound freedom from my mother's control. Any child that leaves home for college is typically faced with a similar soul-searching opportunity. However, my situation was materially different than the typical college freshman spiritual struggle for two specific reasons. Firstly, I was required to participate in something, whereas many new college students choose to default into a spiritual wasteland once they are free from their parents' influence. Secondly, my religious background was far from homogeneous.

Most children are raised in the religion of their parents. Rare are the parents that actively encourage their children to engage in spiritual exploration, let alone support children that may gravitate towards a religion different than that of their parents. This is natural and I'm not criticizing the tendency of parents to try to exert what they see as a positive moral influence on their children. The alternative in most parents' minds would be subjecting their children to the shifting and fickle influences of secular society at too young of an age. Of course, there are those parents that are either agnostic or atheistic and raise their children towards those philosophies as well. The point is that children typically absorb this upbringing and either gravitate towards their parents' belief system, or they gravitate towards a more secular lifestyle. A third option of exploring different churches and belief systems and then selecting which one they think is the best fit for them is typically not considered.

I attended a wide variety of churches during my childhood years, but I cannot attribute it to a desire my mother had to expose me to different belief systems to help me be more spiritually informed. Both of my parents were members of the Church of Jesus Christ of Latter-

Day Saints at the time of my birth. However, once my father passed away when I was only 2 years old, my mother took a more liberal approach to her Christianity. Whatever church we happened to be attending at the time was highly dependent on a number of factors. If my mother was able to secure employment as the church choir director, organist, or pianist, then it was highly likely we would attend that church, regardless of what denomination it was. If my mother had friends at a particular denomination, then we might switch over to that one. A third factor was how likely the pastor was to let my mom perform regular musical pieces, as she enjoyed showcasing her talents in church settings on a regular basis. If a particular pastor chose to keep the focus on God and not have the services turned into a personal talent show for my mother from time to time, then she would move on to a different church. Following this pattern, we attended services of a variety of flavors, including Methodist, Baptist, Lutheran, Presbyterian, Evangelical, LDS, Pentecostal, Episcopalian, and other various non-denominational congregations. Throughout my attendance at Brophy, I was also able to attend regular Catholic mass and get a feel for the Catholic approach to Christianity. All of these denominations fall under the Christianity umbrella, so one could argue that my religious experience wasn't all that diverse after all. However, all of these denominations had differences in their beliefs that at least got me thinking about what made sense to me and what did not.

With this religious background and the spiritual emancipation I felt from leaving my mother's influence, I felt a new sense of religious freedom. I felt free to choose a new approach to my own spirituality, to make that decision based on my experience attending all those different denominations, and to decide based on which one I felt was right for me. I also recalled a special and personal spiritual experience during my sophomore year that had me leaning towards a specific religion. A year prior to entering the boys' home, I was playing an arcade game in a pizzeria in northern Phoenix. A young man I hadn't seen since my time at Royal Palm Junior High approached me while I was playing my game.

After briefly catching up, he said with a smile on his face, "So, I heard a nasty rumor that you're LDS."

His words stirred some memories in the back of my mind, as I had been to so many different churches over the past several years. I had been baptized as a member of the Church of Jesus Christ of Latter-Day

Saints when I was 8 years old, but I had also been baptized as a Baptist at the age of 11.

"I used to be, but not anymore," I replied.

"Well, we have a youth activity this Wednesday at 7pm, we're gonna have a lot of fun – you should come!"

"I'll ask my mom, maybe I'll see you there," I responded.

My mother agreed to take me to the activity as long as I could find a ride home. She dropped me off at an LDS church building in northern Phoenix, and I made my way inside. The doors were open, but it seemed pretty quiet inside, definitely lacking the noise one would expect from a youth activity. There were a few meetings taking place in various rooms, but no sign of any youth. There was a phone hanging on the wall, so I decided to give the guy that invited me a call, to figure out what was going on. His older sister picked up and I told her the situation:

"He's not here right now, he's out with some friends," she responded.

"Well, he invited me to a youth activity, and I'm here at the church building, but there's no activity here," I said.

"Oh, that youth activity got canceled, he must have forgotten to tell you. I'm so sorry!" she replied.

"My mom dropped me off, but she can't pick me up, so I don't have a ride home. How am I supposed to get home?" I asked.

"I can come pick you up and bring you home, but it will take me 10 or 15 minutes to get there," she said.

I thanked her and hung up the phone, feeling annoyed with the whole situation. With some time to kill while I waited for my ride, I started wandering the halls of the church building, admiring the religious artwork decorating the walls. As I casually stopped to take in another painting, I suddenly felt as if someone was quietly but sharply whispering into my mind, "This is your home." A flurry of emotions overwhelmed me in the following moments. I was a bit stunned by the experience, which at the time seemed a bit supernatural to me. My ride eventually showed up, and I returned home without relating the experience to my mother.

Recalling this spiritual experience once I was at the boys' home helped me finalize my decision as I pondered which church I would start attending. After a lot of deliberation, I decided to rejoin the Church of

Jesus Christ of Latter-Day Saints, and I have remained with that religion to this day. My point in sharing this spiritual journey is not to advocate for any one religion over another. Rather I think it's informative for all people to recognize if the spiritual aspect of their lives is on autopilot, or if they are taking a conscientious approach to their spirituality. It has been fascinating for me to meet so many intelligent, accomplished, and highly-ambitious people over the course of my life, while seeing the care and effort they put into their careers juxtaposed with their lackadaisical approach to spirituality. For most people, religion doesn't pay the bills like a career does and is not enjoyable as a source of entertainment, comfort, or ease. However, spirituality is an important aspect of the identity of the whole individual, and it can definitely take a more center stage role as people enter phases of life where a career may be less of a focus.

Joining a fresh congregation as a teenager without any family attending with me was a challenge. Many religions highlight the importance of the family, and as a fresh entrant into a boys' home, the concept of 'family' for me had been turned on its head. Songs like 'Families Can Be Together Forever' were more likely to bring me to tears rather than help me develop an appreciation for family. In one particular youth church class, each teenager had brought one of their parents to class and stood up in front of the class to talk about how much they appreciated them. I couldn't stand to stay there for the duration of that one and had to quietly slip out early while holding back the tears. It took a number of months for me to come to terms with my unique family situation and to develop some friendships with children my age in the congregation. Rather than focusing on the dysfunctional status of my family at the time, I resolved to have my own family one day where I would do things right. Nine kids and twenty-two years of marriage later, I can confidently say that I have become the successful husband and father I aspired to become, and our home, while far from perfect, does operate on a healthy dose of love and peace.

7

AUSTRALIAN BIG WAVE ASPHYXIATION

When I was 16 in the summer of 1995, I had the opportunity to go on a trip to Hawaii and Australia with several high school classmates and a few teachers. We spent 4 days in Honolulu and 17 days in Australia. I was living in the boys' home at the time and didn't have money to pay for the trip fee, which amounted to thousands of dollars. However, an anonymous donor paid for all expenses and gave me $500 spending money as well, with the only request being that I write an essay about the experience once it was all done. Even after returning from the trip and writing the essay as asked, I never did learn the identity of the anonymous donor.

I always loved bodyboarding as a teenager. I learned how to bodyboard at Huntington Beach in Orange County and Mission Beach in San Diego. However, I never had the chance to learn how to surf. Learning how to surf was something I was always enamored with, since as a child I would watch big wave surfers on TV with awe. The opportunity to learn how to surf came during the Honolulu portion of our trip, since one of the teachers on the trip was an avid surfer. I rented a long board and after several failed attempts, I managed to stand up on the board on the waves of Waikiki Beach. The waves weren't that big, and they were very crowded. Someone told me that the big waves come on the North Shore of Oahu in the winter time, and I was on the South Shore in the summer time. These waves were probably about 3 to 5 feet tall, which was big enough for a beginner surfer. However, I naïvely had my sights on trying some bigger waves, in spite of my lack of experience.

On our way from Hawaii to Australia, we had extended layovers in Fiji and New Zealand. While in New Zealand, they had a large sailboat on display, commemorating the fact that New Zealand had just defeated the U.S. in the America's Cup sailing competition that year. While hanging out at a local mall, there was a bit of a commotion as three men

88

slowly strolled through the crowd. All three were in black-colored sports clothing. The one in the middle was about my size, 6'2" and just under 200 pounds, and he was flanked by two truly enormous ogre-like human beings. I asked a nearby local who they were, and she responded, "Those are members of the All Blacks!" After some additional small talk, I learned the All Blacks were the country's rugby team and how popular rugby was in New Zealand.

We boarded our plane and made the final leg of our journey to Australia. With seventeen days on the eastern coast, we had plenty of time to explore. Gift shops had novelties such as didgeridoos, accessories made out of kangaroo skin, and cheap looking boomerangs. I couldn't figure out the circular breathing technique to make the didgeridoo sound decent. However, we were able to take an official training class on how to throw boomerangs correctly. By the end of the class, we were all able to demonstrate a beginner-level proficiency in throwing the boomerang. We also all received our own boomerang with a functional, working design superior to the cheap knockoffs found in the various gift shops.

We visited a wildlife park featuring kangaroos and crocodiles, among many other creatures. We also took a tour through a rain forest. It's true what they say about everything being more vicious in Australia. Even some trees were mean and animal-like. One type of tree in particular, commonly referred to as the Australian banyan, grows around a host tree until the host tree inside of it dies from lack of sunlight and reduced moisture. A trip through the wildlife park showcasing all the reptiles and unusually large insects convinced me that I would never want to settle down in Australia. However, upon exiting the rain forest tour, we ended up in a small grove of trees brimming with small, brightly-colored red and blue birds, slightly larger than a parakeet. These birds were extremely friendly, flying out of the trees and landing on people's heads, shoulders, and hands, as people approached the trees with a small amount of birdseed, which was available from nearby vendors.

For one of the days of the trip, each student stayed with a different host family in Brisbane to learn more about Australian culture and traditions. We played snooker and watched rugby, while the family explained the differences between traditional rugby and the 'aussie rules' format. While outside we could hear a butcherbird singing in the distance. The dinner we shared with them took hours and was much more of a social affair than I was used to in the United States. They had an unusually large number of deadbolt locks on their back door. I asked them what that was all about, and they explained that their backyard went all the way to a swamp area that was populated with crocodiles. During the night the crocodiles would come up to houses and whip their tails against doors to try to get into houses. The next day we visited an Australian high school, and noticed dozens of large fruit bats hanging from the trees on school grounds. By then I was convinced that living in that country must be an ongoing nightmare.

We also traveled to Cairns and took a large hydrofoil boat out to the Great Barrier Reef for snorkeling and scuba diving. They had a scuba diving instructor showing people how to use the scuba gear, but I decided to keep it simple with a plain snorkeling kit. I found that if I held my breath and stuck a finger in the snorkel blow hole, I could then dive down and enjoy the intense, fluorescent colors that the Great Barrier Reef had to offer. Others were doing the same, and we had a decently sized group casually exploring the reef. While snorkeling I went around a corner in the reef and suddenly found myself face to snout with a sand tiger shark. I didn't know what type of shark it was at the time; all I knew was that I was about a foot away from a 9-foot long scary-looking shark, and I panicked violently. The shark turned and swam away, and I made my way to the surface of the water. After relating the experience to one of the boat staff, they said not to worry, that sand tiger sharks typically don't attack humans.

We went to a place called Surfer's Paradise, and I thought for sure I was going to get some big wave surfing opportunities there. However, the water was pretty calm while we were there, so my big-wave surfing aspirations were frustrated yet again. We went to the Hard Rock Café while we were there and otherwise enjoyed our time in a city that seemed like a giant amusement park.

The final city we visited is called Noosa, and we arrived there in the late afternoon. We could see the water from our hotel balcony, and conditions didn't look that interesting from a surfing perspective. We walked into town, which was small and charming, and I was intrigued by the large platforms resting atop the street lights. It turns out that the perches are for pelicans, and it's best not to walk directly beneath these perches. Whenever we saw one of these perches above a street light, directly beneath the perch would be a small, steaming, conical mound of pelican droppings. The sizes of these piles suggested that municipal workers were rarely on pelican dropping cleanup patrol. We walked back to our hotel, and the teachers outlined the remainder of the trip as follows: we would wake in the morning and go visit a nearby beach, before boarding our bus for Sydney, where we would catch our flight home. There would be no sightseeing in Sydney prior to our departure.

That evening I was lamenting the fact that I had yet to see any big waves, in spite of all the wonderful experiences I had had on the trip up to that point. Throughout the trip I had this expectation that I would be able to see some big waves in action and maybe even try to catch one with my newfound surfing skills. Now it was looking like that wasn't going to happen – as a boy who spent most of his life in landlocked Phoenix, it felt like this might be my only shot to experience real surfing. I went to bed that evening after coming to terms with my disappointment, realizing I should have been more grateful for the total experience.

I woke up to the sounds of our balcony doors slightly banging. I stepped out onto the balcony and tried to catch a glimpse of the water as I had done the afternoon before, but there was a heavy fog preventing my view. The weather seemed stormy in a way I had not seen before. After a short period of time, one of the teachers came by to collect us for our walk to the beach before catching the bus. There were some buildings obstructing our view of the beach, and the first thing I saw was a lifeguard tower that was unusually high up off the ground. A few short moments later I caught glimpse of the water, and I realized why the tower was so high.

I finally had my big waves! However, these were not clean looking waves, like you see on TV. The sea was not happy, and the waves were coming in fast and violent. I was not familiar with the technicalities of measuring waves, but the teacher that was a veteran surfer said they were coming in around 22 feet high. There were 2 or 3 surfers (that looked like in more orderly conditions they would have known what they were doing) in bright-colored wetsuits out where the big waves were breaking, but even they were getting clobbered. Our surfer teacher also claimed he could spot a dangerous rip current going out to sea resulting from the storm. If someone were facing the water, there was a lengthy jetty of black, sharp-looking rocks to the right, going out far enough that the large waves were breaking right onto the end of the jetty.

The two teachers offered some precautionary words and said they were okay with us getting in the water briefly, as long as we stayed close to the beach. A few of the students went to rent some bodyboards. The water closest to the beach wasn't too choppy. Going further out to sea, the water gradually started to succumb to very heavy swells, before getting to the point where the large waves were breaking. I got into the water and was playing with my classmates, with my back to the large waves. After a short period of time, I noticed that I was somehow the farthest from the beach of all my classmates, and the swells were getting more powerful. Upon realizing this, I turned around to see what was going on behind me. I was getting closer to the heavy swells, and I suddenly became aware of a subtle yet powerful force that was moving my body farther away from the beach. By the time I realized what was going on, the rip current had dragged me further into the heavy swell section. If I knew then what I know now, I would have stayed calm and tried to swim parallel to the beach towards the jetty. At the time, I just panicked and started trying to swim to shore, but the swells were so large and the rip current was so powerful that my efforts had no effect.

After a short period of struggling, the forces of the heavy swells and the rip current gave way to a much more powerful force, as I was pulled into the first of a number of these big waves. For a moment I felt the excitement that perhaps a big-wave surfer might feel, as I was a part of this tremendously large wave. However, that excitement was figuratively and literally drowned out once the top of the wave plunged me into the water. After some violent tumbling and a desperate scramble for the surface of the water, I made it up for air. Unfortunately, the waves were coming so quickly that as soon as I made it to the surface for air, I was already being pulled into the next big wave, only to be followed again by some violent underwater thrashing. This repeated several times, and the net effect was that I wasn't getting enough air before being plunged back into the water. I was completely exhausted and oxygen-deprived, and I was starting to lose hope as I came up for air for what I thought would be the last time. However, as I came up for air, one of my classmates, appeared right next to me, grabbed my hands in his, and grabbed his bodyboard firmly, sandwiching my hands between his and the bodyboard.

The following wave shot us forward into the heavy swells section. I don't know how he managed to get out to me, but I marveled at his physical ability to rescue me, as I was much taller and heavier than him, and he was a scrawny sophomore. Once in the heavy swell section, he asked, "Man, are you okay? You don't look so good!" We kind of floated along a bit, as we drifted closer to the jetty. As we got closer, he let go of my hands and swam to the jetty and scrambled up the rocks, thinking that I would follow him. Unfortunately, I was too weak to pull myself up out of the water quickly enough, and I was soon pulled back into one of the waves breaking on the jetty. This powerful wave lifted me up and slammed me down onto the rocks. This was exquisitely painful, and I sustained a number of cuts from the impact. I was already exhausted from struggling with the waves for so long, so I just lay there on the rocks. Another wave crashed on me and moved me around a bit, and when the water had filtered down through the rocks, I looked up and saw that a rather large, sharp rock was inches away from my head – I had barely missed having my skull smashed. The adrenaline of this realization shocked me, and I somehow found some additional strength to scramble up the rocks away from where the deadly waves were breaking.

It was at this point that a number of classmates had finally made their way to the end of the jetty to support me as I limped back towards the beach. My classmates and teachers were of course deeply concerned about the near-death experience they had just witnessed, and the teachers were kind enough to not lay into me with 'I told you so' comments. However, their concern and care was limited by the urgency we had in making it to our bus in time to catch our flight from Sydney to Los Angeles.

Some people encounter a 'life flashing before their eyes' type event when they have a near-death experience. When I felt like I wasn't getting enough oxygen, I thought to myself, "What have I done to deserve to die so young?" After that question came to mind, I did actually find my mind rapidly scrolling through a number of visual memories of bad decisions I had already made in my youth. After all of those images flashed through my mind, I quickly came to the conclusion that, yes, I did indeed deserve to die young. I'm grateful that the classmate that rescued me, perhaps with help from a higher power, disagreed with my

logic and gave me a second chance at life.

8

THE MOOSILAUKE RAVINE LODGE

During my high school years at Brophy College Preparatory, the school employed a Harvard man whose primary role was to place the most talented students into the most prestigious colleges. Every year the school would reliably send a group of students to Ivy League institutions. However, some of these students required a little bit of a nudge, to aim higher with their aspirations, and to keep the school's statistics looking good as an Ivy League feeder institution. I was one of those kids.

After I received word that I got a perfect score on the math portion of the SAT, I felt a level of swagger and confidence that I had never felt before. However, I lacked direction and had no short list of colleges that I was targeting in particular. The gentleman in charge of placing talented students into the Ivy League caught me in the hall and pulled me into his office for the first time.

"Jason, where are you applying?" he casually asked.

"My application to the University of Arizona is complete. I also finished an application to MIT and already had an unusually long interview with them. I'm also in the middle of an application to Duke," I replied.

After an unusually long period of silence, during which it felt as if he were peering into my soul, he calmly but firmly stated, "You're going to Dartmouth."

I sat there in brief stunned silence, wondering where this guy I had just met for the first time got the gall to tell me where I would be spending the next four years of my life. While I was still processing his words, he suddenly picked up the phone and dialed a number that I could tell was familiar for him.

"Hey, it's Tom. I'm gonna need you to mail me one of your early decision applications. Thank you." This was before the time of online applications, so we had to wait for the paper application to arrive after he requested it.

While he was on the phone, I was able to regain my composure and ask him a few questions. My first question caught him off guard, as I think he expected the high-performing seniors to already know of him and what he did.

"What do you do here?" I asked.

He explained the close relationships he had with all the Ivy League institutions and his role in maintaining and improving the high school's reputation with those institutions. Then I gave him the question that was really troubling me.

"Why are you so confident that I belong at Dartmouth?" I asked.

"Each one of the Ivy League institutions has its own personality and culture. Even though this is your first time meeting me, I have looked into your accomplishments here at Brophy. Based on what you've done here, I think you'd be very happy at Dartmouth," he responded. I didn't know it at the time, but he was right. I applied to Dartmouth by their early decision deadline and was admitted.

Being accepted in the early decision round reduced the academic pressure of the second semester of my senior year. With more free time, I was able to take on more jobs at the priests' residence as part of my scholarship to attend Brophy free of charge. The man in charge of students working for their tuition made it clear to me that I was no longer working down a balance. As long as I remained eager to help and was willing to be on call for odd jobs that came up, they would consider my debt paid. I was more than happy with this arrangement. On my last day at the boys' home before flying to New England, I decided to shave my head with a razor as a symbol of the new journey I was starting.

The Dartmouth Outing Club does a program before classes start called First-Year Trips. It was billed as a quick way to enjoy the New England landscape and make new friends at the college. I chose to participate in a lengthy canoe trip. We were driven up to Maine and then over the course of four days started canoeing our way back towards the college. Our group included two upperclassmen and several incoming freshmen, all roughly evenly split between boys and girls. The experience culminated with festivities at the Moosilauke Ravine Lodge, a large wood cabin big enough to hold group activities that is owned by the college. The lodge is about a one-hour drive northeast of the college and is truly in the backwoods of New Hampshire.

One of the main activities at the lodge was square dancing the night away on the second floor of the lodge. After working up a sweat, I decided to go out to the balcony to get a breath of fresh air. The moon and stars were clearly visible that night and the air was crisp. I leaned on the railing to enjoy the moment and soon after heard the balcony door open behind me.

"Hey, I was wondering where my dance partner went!"

It was one of the freshmen from my canoe trip, the girl with a very French-sounding name.

"Hey! It was getting a bit stuffy in there, so I just came out for a breather," I replied.

She walked right up next to me and leaned on the balcony railing with me in silence for a few moments.

"Isn't the moon gorgeous tonight?" I asked and then almost immediately cringed at how cheesy I must have sounded.

"It is," she quietly replied, before we both went back to our mutual silence.

Earlier in the day when it was still light, a group of us had gone to the creek not too far from the lodge to take in the scenery. I started paying attention to the subtle sounds of the night and suddenly became aware of the casual trickling of the creek. It was then that I got a crazy idea and slowly turned my head towards her to talk. I noticed as I turned towards her that she almost simultaneously turned her head towards mine and leaned in ever so slightly, bringing our faces quite close to each other. In hindsight, I realized that moment would have been perfect for me to kiss her and start my first romantic relationship in college before classes had even started. However, my romantic cluelessness wouldn't be cured until four years later when I would meet my wife, so the following hilarity ensued instead:

"Are you thinking what I'm thinking?" I gently asked.

"Yes!" she replied with a tender smile on her face and a slight amount of excitement. Not too long after this exchange, I would find out that what she was thinking was without a doubt completely different from what I was thinking.

"All right, let's go!" I said as I headed towards the balcony door, before suddenly stopping and turning to her, "Wait!"

I realized that we weren't going to be able to exit the lodge unless we had a plan. The first floor of the lodge was only accessible via one set of stairs, and there were two upperclassmen positioned at the bottom of the stairs, making sure that all the incoming freshmen stayed on the second floor.

"We'll have to go down separately and be sure to give different excuses," I strategized. However, in our haste, we did not work out our excuses before we set the whole thing in motion.

I headed down first and was abruptly confronted by the two upperclassmen.

"One of my dance partners was complaining about my breath, so I need to go brush my teeth," I said.

The upperclassman squinted his eyes, like part of him didn't believe the excuse I was giving, and then his grin cracked into a crooked smile, as if he knew something was afoot but was willing to let it play out. "Okay, go ahead, but don't be gone long!"

I headed just outside of the lodge's main entrance, waiting for my companion and hoping that she was as successful as I was in getting past the stair guards. A few minutes later, she emerged from the main entrance, and we both involuntary giggled at how mischievous we thought we were being.

"What did you tell them to get past them?" I asked.

"I told them I needed to brush my teeth!" she responded.

"What?? That's the excuse that I used! Wow, I'm surprised that worked. Whatever, we escaped, let's get out of here!" I replied.

I took her by the hand and we excitedly headed down the hill towards the log cabins where we'd all be sleeping later that night. We could have taken our time, but we were both skipping along at a hurried pace, as if time were running out on our fun. Once inside our cabin, I was going to head towards my bunk when she pulled me by the hand in a different direction.

"This way, my bed's over here," she said. It was completely dark with no apparent overhead lighting, so we were bumping into things and feeling our way around for a bit. She fished an electric lantern out of her pack and turned it on, setting it on a small table next to her bed. She then reclined in her bed, while reaching for me.

I stood there for a second, trying to process what was happening, then blurted out, "Um, what are you doing?"

"Are we gonna do this?" she asked. My ignorant question and hesitance immediately put a damper on her cheerfulness, as a look of mixed anticipation and confusion set in on her face.

It wasn't until that moment that I realized her intentions were much different than mine. Not wanting to make her feel bad in an already awkward situation, I tried to explain myself.

"I was thinking we'd grab towels and go take a quick dip in the creek, but now that I think about it, I didn't pack any swim trunks," I said sheepishly.

A look of disappointment crossed her face, but she quickly recovered, apparently not wanting the playfulness we had shared to come to such a quick end.

"And I didn't pack a swimsuit," she replied, "but we can just go in our underwear."

"Okay, but it's a little chilly out there, so let's keep our clothes on until we get to the creek," I replied. We both grabbed towels and dry underwear from our packs and headed out.

We walked down to the creek at a much slower pace than when we were headed to the cabin. We brought the electric lantern with us, but we decided to turn it off and just walk in the moonlight, which was quite bright that night. Once we arrived at the creek, the sounds of the night coupled with the moonlit creek were simply sublime. We started taking our clothes off, and the chill of the night was offset by the warmth I was feeling towards her, in spite of rebuffing her advances in the cabin. Now that she was down to her underwear, seeing her form bathed in the moonlight became a bit too much for me to handle. She turned to me looking expectantly, but without further discussion I made a beeline for the creek and hopped into an area that looked deeper than the rest.

Immediately upon entering the water I realized I had made a very bad decision. The water was so frigid that it felt like my body was going into shock, and the only thing I could think about was getting out of the water as soon as possible. A moment later she hopped in, at which point I immediately got out, with my body no longer able to handle the extreme cold of the creek. She let out a high-pitched yelp as she plunged into the creek and quickly got out herself. With our bodies cold and wet in the chill night air, we both immediately went for our towels and started drying off.

The towels weren't helping with our frosty, wet underwear, so we both headed for the dry underwear we brought. She turned the electric lantern back on and set it on a fallen tree on the bank. While I was still nervously thinking about how to change without her seeing me naked, she took off all her wet underwear and started drying herself off while facing me and looking at me. I just stood there motionless watching her, as I felt paralyzed in the moment, and which she didn't seem to mind. However, once she finished with her towel, I thought she would have headed for her dry clothing to get dressed and warm up after the chilly experience we just had. Instead, she seemed to have a different idea of how to warm up. She laid her towel on the fallen tree and took a couple steps towards me. While still in my cold, wet underwear, I suddenly sensed a firm warning in my mind, which could only have come from my moral subconscious, just one word, but felt in a strong way: "DANGER!" I had attended a variety of churches growing up, but one of the moral principles that had stuck with me was the approach of not having sex before marriage.

I sprang into action, and without turning around, I quickly dropped my wet underwear, grabbed my dry underwear from the fallen tree, put those on, and then continued dressing quickly. A look of disappointment slowly came across her face, and she slowly headed back to her pile of clothing to get dressed as well. We dropped off our wet clothing, towels, and electric lantern at the cabin, and then headed back to the lodge in silence.

A year later, while on my mission to Hungary, I regaled the tale to a group of male missionaries in Budapest. After finishing the story, one of the older missionaries said, "The level of moral strength you demonstrated during that encounter in resisting her advances is atypical for young men. Most guys would have responded very differently and made some poor decisions that evening. I think your new nickname is going to be Mighty Oak, as a symbol of your moral strength." While I have made plenty of mistakes in my life and am far from perfect, I accepted the nickname with pride and always felt a tinge of moral self-confidence when someone referred to me by the nickname. Years have come and gone, and the nickname is no longer in use, but it now serves as a memory of a good decision made on a chilly New England fall evening.

9

THE DARTMOUTH BOATHOUSE

After returning from my canoeing trip, I started getting settled in my dorm room and getting to know my new Freshman year roommate, whom I will call Greg. His parents were divorced and his mother was a wealthy interior decorator. We were very different people but managed to get along quite well and have a lot of fun together. I would occasionally rent an electric guitar from a local music shop called Hanover Strings, and he was very tolerant of my repeated playing of Black Hole Sun by Soundgarden. Our upperclassman resident advisor was less understanding and threatened noise complaints on multiple occasions. Our dorm cluster was called the Choates and was quite far from the main part of campus. The dorm cluster was also considered one of the lowest quality dorms on the entire campus. As such, claiming to live in the Choates was usually accompanied by a snicker. Living that far from the campus also created logistical problems, particularly during the subzero-temperature months of the year.

Greg's academic interests started out in the areas of classics and humanities. I enrolled in a new program called Integrated Mathematics and Physical Sciences (IMPS), hoping that the program, in conjunction with my exceptional math skills, would help me discover a suitable major to focus on later in college. The program was in its first year, so we were in effect the guinea pigs of the masterminds of the program. The philosophy behind the program was that all of the different mathematical and scientific fields of study actually share a lot in common, and synergies could be realized by students that would take classes in all these core scientific subjects simultaneously. However, the execution of the program was flawed in that all of the students in the program felt like they were perpetually drowning, but the professors and administrators of the program were too arrogant to admit these shortcomings and take corrective action in a timely manner.

Rather than doubling down with a determination to do well in an unusually challenging program, I found a new passion to devote my time and energy to that had absolutely nothing to do with my grades and education. The quad on Dartmouth's campus is referred to as 'The Green'. At the beginning of any school year, various clubs and sports organizations would set up little displays on the Green in order to attract new members. While walking on the green one day, I noticed a peculiar-looking long, skinny boat on display, surrounded by some thug-looking upperclassmen that were eyeballing freshman males as they walked by. I would find out later that they were looking for specific body types to recruit as walk-ons for the crew team. My 6'2" frame was muscular, lean, and included an unusually long torso and powerful quadriceps. I also had strong endurance from my three years of long-distance track in high school. All of these attributes would make for a strong walk-on for the heavyweight crew team. They could see hints of these attributes in my frame as I casually walked by, and two of them trotted over to greet me and bring me over to the boat. They spoke briefly about rowing generally and about the Dartmouth Rowing Club specifically. I felt drawn to the program and could see myself becoming an exceptional rower, even though I had no intention of becoming a professional rower after college. I took their flyer regarding the initial club meeting and went on my way.

Days later upon showing up at the initial meeting, I was struck by how many young men showed up to demonstrate their interest in rowing. The Freshman heavyweight coach quieted down the large group and began the meeting.

"I won't cut a single one of you. In the coming weeks, you will cut yourselves," he yelled out to the crowd.

He continued describing the opportunity and gave us all a tour of the rowing tanks and the ergometer room in the gym. Over the coming weeks, his prediction came true. The practices were intense, and one by one the young men that showed up at the initial meeting stopped coming. One of my IMPS program classmates was one of those casualties.

"I'm going to switch over to the rugby club. I've heard their practices are a little less brutal," he whispered to me during class one morning. This same young man would go on to become the head coach of the U.S. national rugby team.

I stuck through the initial phase of the culling, but the difficulty only increased from there. We started doing double practices on Saturdays, and I had to start eating 5 full meals per day just to provide my body with enough calories to burn in our difficult practices. Due to my challenging homework load, I started getting less sleep, and my grades started to suffer. However, I remained committed to the crew team.

I became friends with one of my crew teammates who was from Lexington, MA. He rowed in high school and was an impressive 6'7" in height, giving him a strong advantage on the team. I didn't have any plans to return to Arizona for the Thanksgiving holiday, so this friend invited me to join him and his family for the occasion. Over the course of our friendship, I had learned that he was an only child, and he had spent his entire childhood living a wealthy New England lifestyle. Upon arriving at his home, I met his parents for the first time, and they gave me a tour of the house. Prominently placed on an ornate coffee table in the living room was an oversized, colorful book celebrating homosexuality in America. I didn't think much of it in the moment, but later that evening it got me thinking, is my new friend gay? The next day, we went over to a family friend's house with a similar family structure: mom, dad, and one son that was also college aged. I started noticing some unusual interactions between my new friend and the son at this new house. I started putting the pieces together and realized that my new friend was indeed gay. Having a gay friend was a new experience for me, and I didn't know how to internalize it or what the appropriate boundaries would be in such a relationship. Upon our return to campus, I started telling a few of our rowing teammates in confidence that my new friend on the team was gay. At the time, I didn't realize that I was 'outing' him and how inappropriate that behavior was. My gossip was met with disbelief at first by those that I told. Unfortunately, word seemed to get out about his sexual orientation, and our friendship quickly faded once he realized that I was the culprit.

The Dartmouth Rowing Club used to host a winter formal dance, where the male and female rowers would bring dates to a dance in the boathouse. It was considered one of the special traditions of the College, and it was considered an honor to be invited to the dance by a member of the crew team. I had been writing my high school girlfriend on a weekly basis for several weeks, hoping that we could somehow maintain a long-term relationship. However, she had started talking about dates she had with other guys, so that tipped me off that she was moving on with her life, and I probably should, too. Before getting serious about who I would take to the dance, I decided to have a little bit of fun with my roommate.

My roommate was below average height and of weak stature, and like many freshmen lacked confidence when it came to interacting with women. However, he had met a special someone, and their relationship was at that point right before they got serious and exclusive. Just to be a jerk, I decided to ask this girl that he was so focused on to my crew formal. I thought asking her would be enough to get him riled up, and I never expected her to accept the invitation. To my surprise she accepted the invite with enthusiasm and sincerity! I didn't think this would happen, and then I had a decision to make. On the one hand, I had to somehow break it to her that I wasn't interested in her, and that I was just asking her to the dance to mess with my roommate. Secondly, my roommate found out that I had invited her and she had accepted, which led to a particularly fiery altercation between the two of us. With almost a look of madness in his eyes, he looked me dead on and said, "Jason, I will kill you." I didn't take him for a murderer, but he made it very clear that I had crossed the line. I got the intended effect of making him mad, and then explained to him that I was just doing it to mess with him. After a while, he calmed down, and we had a good laugh about it later. Years later they would end up getting married.

There were two girls that I was primarily interested in during my freshman year. One was a junior, and we would meet up once or twice per week to make music together or just hang out. I wasn't particularly attracted to her, but I had fun hanging out with her, and I considered it more of a friendly relationship. The other was a short but cute LDS freshman. I worked up the courage to ask her out and picked up my dorm room phone. At this point it's important to mention that Dartmouth had a program called Blitzmail that was an early version of email, but the students almost used it like texting in the mid-90's. I had no version of email or texting in high school, so this new form of communication was an exciting new development for freshman back then. Everybody used it to communicate, and most dorm room phones went unused collecting dust. However, I thought asking her out via Blitzmail was too lame, so I decided to use the dorm phone.

"Helloooooooo…?" she answered with a confused tone.

"Hey, it's Jason! How are you?" I responded with a nervous, forced cheerfulness.

"Nobody has EVER called me on this phone," she replied.

After some additional small talk, I invited her to the dance. To my delight she accepted, and then I left her with a parting request.

"Oh, I almost forgot. Be sure to bring a towel," I said casually.

"Why would I need to bring a towel to a dance?" she asked.

"One of the traditions of the dance is that after people have danced for a bit in the boathouse, they then go down to the dock, take off their clothes in the dark, and jump into the cold river to cool off. Then they dry off and head back up for more dancing. It's completely dark on the dock, so you can't see anything while you're skinny dipping," I responded.

After an uncomfortable period of silence, she replied, "Let's skip that part, and we can go swimming together some other time."

The day came for the dance, and we headed down to the boathouse together. After our night of dancing, I learned an important lesson. My date was attractive, but we had virtually no chemistry. I discovered that having that chemistry was more important to me than the attractiveness of my date.

Once a week, typically on a Monday night, the LDS students at Dartmouth would get together to hang out. The Monday following the dance was such an occasion, and both my dance date and the junior girl I would make music with were at the event. In a way that seemed very sudden and out of nowhere, the junior girl spoke up in front of everyone, saying, "Jason, I could never marry you, because I could never trust you." At first I thought she was joking. However, after some additional conversation, it became evident that she was quite serious. She had developed feelings for me over the course of all our music sessions, and she took it as a betrayal that I had asked the other girl to the dance. I quite honestly had no idea that the junior girl had those kinds of feelings for me. Needless to say, our musical meet ups tapered off shortly thereafter.

I started focusing more on my crew training, spending more time at the boathouse exercising. The dangling carrot I was chasing there was the opportunity to make 'first boat', which consisted of the 8 best members of the freshman heavyweight crew team. In spite of being a walk on and not having any high school experience with rowing, like some of my teammates, I still felt like I had a chance if I worked hard enough. However, that dream and all the hard work that went into it seemed to fade away when I came down with a case of walking pneumonia. I was sidelined from workouts for several weeks, and at one point I thought I was going to just have to quit crew due to how far behind I fell while sick. However, once I started feeling better, I started missing being with the team and being on the water. I decided to return to practice, even though I felt like my chances at making first boat had been dashed.

During the winter time, the Connecticut river adjacent to the Dartmouth campus completely freezes over, making rowing impossible for a number of months. In order to get some practice in the boat, colleges that have their water sources frozen during the winter like this typically travel for some sort of spring training. We did the same and traveled down south to a small town called Clinton, TN. There were a number of buffet style restaurants near the river where we were training, which felt like heaven to us calorie-crunching, hungry college athletes.

Over the course of our spring training, it became evident that the coach was taking the opportunity to finalize the membership of the first boat. In an exciting turn of events, I found myself in what's called a 'seat race' for the last spot on the first boat. During a seat race, two boats race each other, and the coach records the results. Then the coach switches one person from each boat and repeats the race. The teammate I was competing against was good, but he lacked the intensity that I was able to turn on when needed. I let out an audible shout as I put everything I had into that seat race, and it paid off! I was awarded the final spot in the first boat of our freshman heavyweight crew team in the 1996-1997 school year.

We returned up north, and soon the ice on the Connecticut River started breaking up. As soon as the floating ice chunks were small enough to present less of a risk to damaging our boats, our coach got us back on the water. Even though the ice was breaking up, the water was still extremely cold. The coach was explaining the physics to us that even though the water was in liquid form and moving, it could still be at sub-freezing temperatures. It was on one of these early days that we actually managed to tip our 8-man sweep boat, which is quite difficult to do actually and doesn't happen that often unintentionally. We all fell into the subfreezing water, and the coach quickly brought his small boat around to start picking us up a couple at a time. Because of my position in the boat, I was one of the last to be picked up and therefore had one of the longest exposures to the freezing cold water. The coach quickly brought us back to the boathouse, and we all ran to the warm showers. After spending a number of minutes under the hot water, my body unfortunately was not warming up, and I was shaking uncontrollably. Fearing that I was going into hypothermic shock, the coach ordered one of my teammates to take me to the campus clinic. I got there and they gave me dry hospital clothing, wrapped me in a blanket, and then literally gave me just a chocolate chip cookie and a hot cocoa. "Seriously? I'm suffering from hypothermia, and you're giving me a blanket and a cookie?" I complained to the clinic staff. "Just drink the cocoa and relax," they reassured me. Sure enough, my body started warming back up and I was fine.

The double practices we were doing on Saturdays were extended to weekdays as well, where we would practice in the early morning before classes started, and then do another one in the late afternoon. I continued neglecting my coursework, and I felt like all of my time was being spent either training, eating, or sleeping, while homework took a back seat. My grades continued to suffer, but I remained focused on crew. I hit a low point one day when I finished a homework problem set but was too tired to stay for the class. I came to class in a full set of pajamas, with other classmates looking on and snickering and in full view of the bewildered professor. Without speaking a word, I put my homework in the completed assignment pile, took the handouts for the day, then turned right back around and walked out. I headed back to my dorm and fell asleep.

However, the intensity I brought to the first boat was shared by my boatmates, and we quickly gained a reputation as having one of the most explosive starts in freshman crew in the country. I was in the best shape of my life and had built quite the physique. We notched up wins against University of New Hampshire, MIT, Syracuse, and others, while losing to Yale and Brown. Columbia sent their varsity team up to Dartmouth to compete against our freshman boat, and we humiliated them in a most satisfying way. We earned a spot to compete at the collegiate rowing national championship, and our boat placed 6th in the nation in the freshman heavyweight 8-man sweep category that year. We might have had a better finish that year if one of our teammates hadn't caught a crab during one of the races. In rowing, catching a crab is when a rower loses control of their oar, thus slowing down the boat slightly. The teammate that caught the crab went on to become the captain of the varsity team a few years later.

The excitement of such a strong finish at nationals was intoxicating. However, as a young man in the LDS faith, I faced a difficult decision. At the time, it was expected that 19-year-old males in the LDS church would typically serve full-time, two-year missions after freshman year. After much thought and spiritual meditation on the subject, I decided that I would serve a mission as well. My aunt offered to buy me a car if I would stay in college and not serve a mission. Also, since I was a solid member of the first boat, the rowing coaches had plans for me on the junior varsity team the following year. However, I made the difficult decision to disappoint my aunt, my coach, and all my friends I left behind in order to serve a mission. Dartmouth's policy towards LDS students that served missions at the time was to force them to reapply if they wanted to come back to Dartmouth two years later, but I decided to take my chances with the mission anyway. With how bad my grades were, I left the beautiful Dartmouth campus thinking that I might not return.

10

AN UNEXPECTED VISITOR

I returned to Phoenix after my freshman year at Dartmouth in order to prepare for my mission. I was still not on good terms with my mother, and the boys' home that I lived in prior to Dartmouth was not able to accommodate program graduates once they were in college. As such, I arranged to live with an elderly couple in the congregation I attended while I lived in the boys' home. I started attending church with that same congregation, and they let me use a small pickup truck one of their sons had left behind to get around for the summer. I also reached out to the President of Brophy, who was instrumental in getting me into the boys' home, to let him know I was back in the Phoenix area and looking for work for the summer. He reached out to Dana Construction, which was a construction firm that did a lot of work for the high school, and they hired me as a carpenter's apprentice.

Carpentry work during the summer in Phoenix was particularly brutal. Working outside in the desert caused me to quickly sweat through all my clothes, and then all the sheet rock dust and sawdust would cling to my exposed sweaty skin, making me thoroughly filthy by the time I got home from work each evening. Being caked in dirt and debris like that and then just hopping directly into the shower led to some plumbing problems about which my hosts were not overly enthused. One day it seemed the lady was on the verge of asking me to hose off in the backyard before hopping in the shower. However, life had a way of solving her plumbing problems without me changing my shower habits, as my job as a carpenter's apprentice did not last the entire summer.

When I started the job, we were primarily working on projects where we were either building a new residential home or heavily remodeling an existing residential home. However, they would work on other odd jobs as they came along, and they decided to put me on one of those. A couple wanted the pool removed from their backyard, and the water had already been drained from the pool. Apparently, the way to remove a pool like this requires a whole lot of jackhammering. I had no experience operating a jackhammer, but the head of the construction company thought he'd put me on the job anyways. Once we arrived at the job site, we headed to the backyard and he started giving me instructions.

"Break the whole pool up into pieces that will be small enough and light enough for us to carry away," he instructed.

"How long will this take?" I inquired.

"You might not get it all finished today, but whatever's left, you can finish it up tomorrow," he replied.

He left me alone at the job site and I started jackhammering. I had a pair of work gloves on, but they had no vibration dampening features. As I continued jackhammering for hours without anybody to relieve me, I started losing feeling in my hands. At first I thought this was just a drawback of this particular kind of job, and I told myself that the construction manager wouldn't put me in a situation that would cause long term damage to any part of my body. However, as the numbness worsened, I started to fear that I was going to sustain long-term damage to the nerves in my hands. I shut off the jackhammer, hopped in my pickup truck, and left the work site. As I headed home, I knew that I would get in trouble with the construction manager for leaving work early like that. However, the more I thought about it, I realized that I didn't want to spend the rest of the summer working construction, so I decided that I would not return to work. Later that evening, I received a call from the construction manager. I could tell from his tone that he was very upset about what I did but was also genuinely curious as to why I left so abruptly.

"You left early before the job was done, son! I had to send someone else over to finish the job! Why did you leave like that?" he asked in a stern tone.

I explained to him the concern with my hands, but then quickly transitioned to letting him know that I wouldn't be returning to work.

The very next Sunday, I let the bishop of our congregation know that I was looking for a summer job now that the construction gig was over. That same day a lawyer in the congregation said he could take me on for the summer to help him with filing and data entry at his law office. I took the job without asking what type of legal work he focused on, or what types of clients he represented. I soon started in his law office in downtown Phoenix and quickly learned some disturbing news. Motorola had been dumping a chemical called TCE into the ground, and this chemical had polluted the two main aquifers in the region. After making its way into the area's drinking water, people in the surrounding vicinity started suffering from ailments related to TCE exposure: birth defects, autoimmune diseases, cancer, and kidney issues. The people rose up and joined a class action lawsuit against the company.

"Please tell me we're representing these poor people that have had their lives ruined by this company," I stated softly to him while looking over some of the papers he had given me.

"My firm is actually representing and defending Motorola in this lawsuit," he responded.

My job ended up more focused on data entry, and the work was heart breaking. In particular each member of the class action lawsuit submitted detailed accounts of the illnesses they and/or their children had contracted from drinking the contaminated ground water. My job was to enter each of these detailed accounts into a computer database. The vast majority of the accounts seemed to be that of childhood leukemia and the resulting side effects of chemotherapy. Sometimes the side effects of the chemotherapy were worse than the symptoms of the leukemia itself. In spite of how emotionally difficult it was to review all of these cases, I decided I wanted to keep the job. I figured out a way to emotionally detach myself from what I was entering into the computer database. I also started paying more attention to my two college-age female coworkers, which served as a pleasant diversion. One of them was a curvy, Polynesian brunette, and the other was petite and towheaded. After a number of weeks with me flirting primarily with the Polynesian girl, she and her friend approached me one day.

"We were thinking the three of us could go to a movie. What do you think?" she asked.

I felt like I had just won the lottery, but I didn't want to seem overly enthusiastic, so I calmly replied with, "That sounds great, let's do it."

We agreed on a date and time, and the girls insisted that they would pick me up in one of their cars. The date happened to be on a day after my last day with the company. When the day came, I headed out to the front curb of the place where I was staying, eagerly waiting for the girls to arrive. However, the girls never showed up. It was my first time being stood up for a date and came as a tremendous disappointment. Since I no longer worked with them and didn't have their phone numbers, I never found out if they stood me up on purpose, or if some emergency came up to prevent them from coming. Regardless, the dream date never materialized.

The bishop of our ward lived just across the street from where I was living, and we had frequent interactions due to my mission preparations. One Sunday morning, as I was driving to church, there was a gorgeous woman in a black bikini washing her car in her driveway. I took in the sight and then continued on my way to church. Later during church services, during a break between meetings, the bishop approached me.

"Hey Jason, on your way to church, did you happen to notice that woman washing her car in her driveway?" he asked me casually.

"Um, yeah, it's kinda hard not to notice something like that," I responded.

"Did you look at her as you drove by?" he continued.

Trying to understand if he was drawing a distinction between 'noticing' and 'looking', I stood there in silence contemplating his question. After a few moments, he could see I was caught up in my thoughts, and he broke the silence.

"As I approached her house, I could tell in my peripheral vision that there was a scantily-clad woman in the driveway. In that moment, as I was driving to church, I made a quick decision that I wasn't going to look at her," he said.

He then went on to explain a common Mormon phrase used in training missionaries, which is "If you don't look once, you're not a man, but if you look twice, you're not a missionary." LDS missionaries are not allowed to date during their years of service, so it requires some mental conditioning to put aside romantic desires and focus on the missionary work.

I had submitted my missionary application papers towards the beginning of the summer, and there tends to be some uncertainty regarding how quickly any particular missionary will receive their assignment. However, the day finally came that my invitation to become a missionary, also known as a 'mission call', arrived in the mail. It's typical for youth to be surrounded by family, and maybe even some close friends, when opening their mission call, but I was not familiar with this tradition. When I received my mission call, I went to my room that evening and opened the envelope alone. After the initial excitement wore off when I saw that I'd be serving in Hungary, I started feeling a deep, painful sadness that I had nobody with whom to share my excitement. I started crying harder than I ever had in my life, and it was that painful type of crying that just hurts you right in the gut. While I was in the depths of this sadness, I suddenly felt a wave of comfort and peace come over me, and I became aware of some sort of strong, spiritual presence in the room with me. To this day I do not know what that presence was, whether it was my deceased father or perhaps something else, but I will never forget that feeling I had when that presence comforted me in the depths of my sadness.

Now that my summer jobs were over and I had received my mission call, I felt I still had some unresolved issues and feelings with how my relationship with my high school girlfriend ended. On a late summer evening, feeling contemplative and in the mood for a bit of a walk, I decided to write a final goodbye letter to my old girlfriend, walk the two miles to her house, hand deliver it, and then walk back home. I got to her house, and her mother answered the door.

"Can you please give this to your daughter?" I asked. "I won't be staying, so I don't need a response from her. Thank you." I handed her the note and then started walking back home. I got about halfway down the street before my high school girlfriend drove up in her car.

"Jason, get in. It's silly to walk all the way back when it's this dark," she protested. I decided to not be overly dramatic about it and got in the car. As she drove me home, she was very kind and communicated to me that even though we were no longer together, she harbored no ill will towards me and had many fond memories of our time together. It was therapeutic hearing those thoughts from her, and it really helped me emotionally move on as I continued to prepare for my mission.

After she dropped me off, I headed into a lesser used family room in the house where I was staying. I thought the elderly couple was asleep at that point in the evening. I took a seat in a high-backed, cushioned chair and just sat there in the dark room for what seemed like half an hour, with thoughts swirling around in my head. All of a sudden, the door between that room and the backyard opened, and in walked the elderly couple, both completely without clothes and still damp from a dip in a pool. As the lady turned the light on, she startled as she saw me sitting quietly in the chair in the corner, and my mouth dropped open as I noticed they were both naked. She quickly moved to cover herself with her arms, and her husband sheepishly hid behind her.

"Jason! I'm so sorry! We thought you were away with friends this evening and didn't expect you home so soon! Bill and I like to take a dip in the pool on hot summer nights occasionally, and when we're done, we leave our wet bathing suits outside and just come inside naked," she explained. Ignoring the fact that they were naked, I explained to them the heart-to-heart conversation I had with my girlfriend, and how I was still caught up in all the emotions of that encounter. Bill scurried off to a different room and I didn't see him for the rest of the evening. However, his wife casually covered herself with a towel and then came over to comfort me, as she could tell that the emotional burden of what I had experienced with my girlfriend that evening was much stronger than seeing them naked.

The time came for my final church services before I headed up to the Missionary Training Center in Provo, Utah. Even though I continued to not be on good terms with my mother, the bishop arranged for her to attend our church services that Sunday. In the LDS church, it is customary to occasionally have special musical pieces played by members of the congregation, but overly flashy music is discouraged, as it tends to bring the focus away from Christ and more towards the expertise of the musician. However, my mother has always been a performer at heart and craves the attention of an audience, even in church settings. The bishop gave her permission to play a flashier piece as part of my farewell services. She chose a piece called 'Doctor Gradus ad Parnassum' by Debussy. I've never heard the song played with such emotion as she played it that day, and it brought me to tears. Later that evening, Bill sat at the piano and started telling me about how he studied piano at Stanford. He tried to play the piece that my mom played, but he technically struggled with it and definitely played it with no emotion. His struggle with the piece made her flawless and emotion-filled performance that day all the sweeter to me.

In that same final church service, an older gentleman in the ward approached me and issued me a challenge for my mission. "I challenge you to read your patriarchal blessing every day of your mission, and I know you will be blessed if you do." In the LDS church, a congregation is typically made up of 300 to 500 members and is called a 'ward'. Several wards are organized into a larger entity referred to as a 'stake'. Each stake has a patriarch who is called to give patriarchal blessings to members of that stake. I had received such a blessing before heading out to Dartmouth, and it contained many precious thoughts of encouragement and guidance. I accepted his challenge, although I worried that it might become burdensome on days where there wasn't enough time to do so. However, little did I know that his challenge would become instrumental in me staying on my mission during a particularly difficult time when I was considering returning home early.

That same evening, Bill's wife pulled me aside to give me some final advice before I headed off for my mission.

"Who are you?" she asked.

I stood there quietly, not knowing how to answer the question, as nobody had ever asked me that question with such a philosophical tone to it.

I gave her my name and a little bit of my background, all of which she knew already.

"No," she said abruptly, cutting me off. "If anybody ever asks who you are, the first thing that should come to mind is that you are a child of God."

After some further discussion, particularly regarding my troubled childhood, she said, "I think you have become very good at surviving, but you don't know how to thrive." At first I took it as an insult that she was pointing out such a major shortcoming in my character, but then I slowly started realizing that there was some truth to her assertion. I started thinking about what it means to thrive in life, and how I would need to change my mindset if I were ever to completely pull myself away from the poor, rugged childhood I had experienced. A year at Dartmouth was a good start, but I realized that the mission would also be transformative, and that a lot of work remained before I could claim that I had learned how to thrive.

11

STOPPED IN OUR TRACKS

It is common but not required for youth of the Church of Jesus Christ of Latter-Day Saints to serve a mission, either right after high school, or while taking a break from college. The mission usually lasts for two years and sometimes takes the youth to a foreign country. Missionary work is heavily focused on religious education and service. It typically has very little in common with the sensationalized, unrealistic, and offensive behavior and dialog depicted in the popular 'Book of Mormon' Broadway hit. However, the two-year experience was exhilarating and formative me, especially after such a raw and tumultuous freshman year at Dartmouth.

For a typical youth mission, the breakdown of the work is probably around 80% proselytizing and 20% service. The proselytizing usually takes the form of warm contacts and cold contacts. Warm contacts include people that have previously shown interest in learning about the church, or referrals where someone has requested to meet with the missionaries. Cold contacts include street contacting (also known as 'streeting') or going door to door (also known as 'tracting'). For streeting, we would typically post up in the town square and try to talk to strangers walking through the area, although streeting could really happen at any time and place, such as public sidewalks, parks, etc. A person that was not a member of the church but interested in learning more about it was referred to as an 'investigator'. Male missionaries had the title of 'Elder' before their last name (e.g., I was 'Elder Merrill'), and the female missionaries had the title of 'Sister' before their last name. The service portion of the mission usually involved meeting and spiritually strengthening existing members, teaching free English classes (for foreign missions only), cleaning up parks and roads, helping people with construction projects, helping out on a farm, etc. The ultimate goal for missionaries was to bring people closer to Christ, and a secondary goal was to increase church membership through conversion. I've done a lot of challenging things in my life, but 'selling' an unusual religion in a foreign country while speaking a foreign language definitely ranks up there as one of the most challenging.

Young men of missionary age go on missions for a variety of reasons. Some feel pressure from their parents to go on a mission, so that they can follow in the footsteps of their grandfather, father and/or older brothers. Parents or grandparents might also offer worldly incentives, such as a car or money for college, to entice the youth to go on missions as well. Some go on a mission out of a sense of spiritual or moral duty to do so. Others see it as a way to gain spiritual and social maturity at a critical time in life. Some young women are raised to prefer young men that have completed a mission (also known as 'returned missionaries' or 'RMs') when selecting a husband, so there can be a 'natural selection' motivator for young men as well. Some also see it as a tremendous opportunity to experience a new culture and learn a new language, which can definitely give perspective and provide depth of character. Others that may have a strong love of the gospel just feel a sense of urgency in sharing that joy with others. For me it was a combination of many of these factors that led me to decide to serve a mission.

After completing two months of Hungarian language and culture training at the Missionary Training Center in Provo, UT, I reported to mission headquarters in Budapest, Hungary. The mission president had a large board showing where the country's missionaries were all stationed, and I was sent to Szombathely (pronounced SOAM-bought-hey) for my first location. Szombathely is a small town in the western part of the country, near the country's border with Austria. My first companion, who was also considered my 'trainer' since I was new, was from Vernal, UT. In an effort to break me in, he took me to a McDonald's and made me order for myself in Hungarian. We of course learned numbers at the Missionary Training Center, but I was new and flustered when the time came for me to order. I accidentally ended up ordering five double cheeseburgers, instead of just the one that I wanted. With a smile on his face, he said that I had to eat all five, since I made the mistake. I could tell he found the situation amusing, but I could also see that he was serious about my punishment.

Other food challenges awaited me as I started to experience some of the unusual cuisine that Hungarians enjoy. One of the most peculiar was a dish called 'kocsonya'. The dish was typically one of the many meals that would result from a 'diszno ölés' (pronounced DEECE-no OO-laysh), which translates to 'pig killing'. In an effort to use as much of the animal as possible, while processing the animal they would collect all the pig fat. This fat would then be boiled until it turned into a liquid, and then various vegetables or meat tidbits would then be added to the boiling fat. This mixture would then be poured into a large, deep dish and put in the fridge. As the dish chilled in the fridge, the mixture would congeal and turn into a sort of pig fat jello. In some cultures, it can be considered very impolite to not eat what is served to you, and Hungarian culture is definitely one of those. I was sensitive to this and didn't want to hurt anybody's feelings. However, the kocsonya dish was the only one on my mission where after I took one bite, I couldn't force myself to eat any more of it, in spite of the pressure and awkward looks that followed.

On another occasion, we were knocking on doors, and a middle-aged woman invited us into her home to chat. After we discussed various religious topics, she invited us to stay for dinner. "How about chicken

147

soup?" she offered, speaking in Hungarian of course. We responded that sounded great, and we stayed seated in the living room for a moment, while she headed towards the kitchen. We then stood up and headed after her into the kitchen in order to offer our help in preparing the meal, but we then realized she made her way through the kitchen and into the backyard. My companion and I casually headed towards the backyard to see what she was up to. Once we reached the back door, we could see the woman in her backyard chasing down one of her many chickens. She brought it over to a wooden table in the backyard and without delay picked up a large cleaver and chopped off its head. She then proceeded to start pulling the feathers off of it, at which point I turned to my senior companion with a look of horror on my face.

"When I said I wanted chicken soup, I didn't mean like THAT!" I whispered in English, as I felt a pit in my stomach. "I didn't think it would be this fresh!"

A while later we all sat down to enjoy the fresh chicken soup she had prepared for us. I took hold of the ladle and peered into the pot as I stirred it, thinking that what was in there was just recently strolling around the backyard, living its best life. As I dipped the ladle in and out of the soup, to my surprise I could see the chicken's head and both of its claws in the soup. I immediately looked up and stared into the distance, trying my best not to throw up. Once the nausea subsided, I once again turned to my senior companion.

"Why are the chicken's head and claws still in the soup?" I whispered in English.

He smiled and whispered, "They say it's for the flavor! Don't be rude, Elder! Eat up!"

I continued to strengthen my Hungarian language skills, but I would still occasionally make mistakes, sometimes embarrassing ones, in front of native Hungarians. The 'F' word in Hungarian is 'basz meg', or sometimes shortened to just 'basz', and it is pronounced like the English word 'boss'. One Sunday we had the zone leader and his companion visiting us, and we were in the foyer of the church building as services had just concluded. The building was bustling with all the native Hungarian church members that were socializing after the church services had ended. The zone leader had gathered all of us missionaries and was explaining his plan for what we would do that afternoon. After he had finished explaining, in an effort to make a joke and lighten the mood, I loudly exclaimed, "Okay, you're the boss!" in front of all the Hungarian church members. The foyer all of a sudden got really quiet as the members turned towards the group of missionaries, staring at me and wondering why a missionary of all people would use the 'F' word on the Sabbath and in the church building.

One weekday per week is designated as 'Preparation Day', or 'P Day' for short. This is the day when missionaries are supposed to do their laundry, clean their apartment, buy groceries, take care of any other errands, and then also squeeze in a little fun, if time permits. On a certain P Day, my companion and I decided to visit the town of Kőszeg, which is not too far from Szombathely. We stopped by a book store once we arrived there, and we were surprised to see a copy of the Hungarian Book of Mormon for sale there. As part of our missionary efforts, we were always happy to give away copies of the Hungarian Book of Mormon for free, so it was disappointing to us that someone was trying to make money by selling one. After we left the bookstore, we noticed some signs advertising an international chess tournament that was open to the public for free viewing. We entered the building and headed towards where the players were, and an attendant reminded us to keep silent as we walked from board to board. To our surprise, there were a number of chess grandmasters and international masters competing at the event. One of the players from Israel was wearing a colorful purple button-down shirt with a few of the top buttons undone and a thick tuft of brown chest hair on display. The player from the United States seemed like a chubby teenager with unwashed hair, listening to a Walkman as he played. As his opponent played a particularly good move, the American stopped bobbing his head to his music and slowly reached over to turn off the Walkman. The tension was as dramatic as it gets in the quiet world of chess.

On a different P-day, a group of us missionaries visited a nearby town called Sopron before heading over to the Austria/Hungary border. The main attraction in Sopron was a castle that a man had been building for himself over the course of decades, and visitors were allowed to tour the premises. As we headed towards the Austria/Hungary border, we came across some deserted Russian military barracks. Hungary was occupied by Russian soldiers and behind the 'Iron Curtain' until 1989. As we walked through the deserted ruins, we couldn't help but feel a sense of overwhelming dread, as the broken, time-worn buildings

151

symbolized the unwelcome communism that was forced upon the Hungarian people for decades.

Upon reaching the border, we came upon what looked like an outpost manned by two young men in Austrian military uniform wielding machine guns. In spite of their imposing weaponry, they waved to us with bright smiles. One of the missionaries in our group spoke German, so he decided to try his luck in communicating with them. He struck up quite the conversation with them and learned a lot about what they were doing. It turns out that they were about the same age as us missionaries, around 19 to 21 years old. Austria at the time required some sort of military service from its young men, and these two young men were completing their required service. We didn't notice any walls or fencing at the border, so our German-speaking companion asked them what exactly their job was. They responded that they were not there to keep Hungarians out of Austria. On the contrary, the biggest problem they had to deal with was Austrians crossing the border into Hungary in order to buy groceries and other essentials at much lower prices, since the two economies were functioning at drastically different levels.

One of the relics of the communist occupation were the large apartment towers that dotted the landscape. These apartment towers were typically around ten stories high, with four apartments per level. The communists liked the format, as the buildings were relatively cheap to build and able to house a large number of people with only a four-apartment footprint from a land use perspective. The Hungarian word for these structures was lakotelep. Two opposing sides of the tower would include windows and balconies, and the other two sides were just flat and featureless. Some clever soul got the idea that these flat tower sides could be used like billboards for advertising. As the practice became more prevalent, they discovered that painted advertisements worked better than wallpapered panels on the sides of these buildings. Painters that were willing to do their work on suspended platforms attached to and lowered from the tops of the towers are the ones that would complete this type of work. We had such a painter in our local congregation, and he considered himself a 'true artist', rather than a simple painter by trade. My companion and I were invited to his home to visit them and share a meal and a gospel discussion. As he had referred to himself as an artist in church before, we expected to see some of his artwork on display upon visiting his home. However, we were not expecting the prominent piece of art that we encountered in their main living room when we arrived. We all sat down to chat, and hanging on the wall behind the painter and his wife was a large, incredibly detailed, and accurate pencil drawing of the painter's wife, fully nude and in a casual, sitting pose. As my eyes darted between the framed drawing and the painter's wife sitting on the couch in front of us smiling, it struck me that it was not a point of awkwardness or embarrassment to either of them. If anything, he seemed proud of both his artistic skill and his wife's excellent physical shape, and he was more than happy to have both on display in the framed piece of art. This was the first of many similar experiences over the course of my two years in Hungary where I learned that Hungarians have drastically different attitudes towards modesty and nudity than we have in the United States.

Another example of this was particularly on display during the summer months. Many Hungarians weren't wealthy enough to have air conditioning units. In order to cope with the heat and humidity of the summer, they would simply lounge either in their underwear or in the nude while at home. It would always come as a surprise to the newer missionaries knocking on doors when the door would be answered by someone in their underwear or even partially nude in some cases. At this point it's relevant to mention that missionaries are not supposed to go on dates or form romantic relationships. This would make it particularly challenging when these sexually-repressed male missionaries would occasionally encounter young women in their underwear while knocking on doors. The typical male missionary response to those types of situations was to show some restraint and try to be professional. However, the mission president's wife was concerned that some male missionaries weren't able to handle these types of situations in an effective manner, but would instead be motivated to move on to the next door rather than engage a gorgeous woman in only her underwear in a thoughtful gospel discussion. This caused her to make the statement to the entire mission that "young, beautiful women need the gospel, too." I tried to take her advice to heart, but when I encountered my first young woman with less clothing than I was used to, I literally froze like a deer in the headlights. She smiled and let out a small laugh as she could tell what effect she was having on me as I stared at her in silence. My senior missionary companion waited patiently for me to regain my composure,

155

but that moment never came. He finally broke the awkward tension and asked the girl if she had ever heard about our church, even though it was definitely my turn to make the introduction at that door.

On a different day, my trainer and I were going from street to street, knocking on doors and talking with people about our church. The sun was out and the weather was calm and comfortable that day. Just as we turned down a new street, at almost the same time we both abruptly stopped walking. I felt as if some unseen powerful force was literally preventing me from taking another step. I turned towards my companion.

"Do you feel that?" I asked, without giving any additional detail.

"Yeah," he responded.

Later that evening, we tried to make sense of what had happened. When it occurred, we looked down the street but didn't see any visible danger. It was early afternoon and the sun was bright. The experience was surreal, but the fact that my companion had felt the exact same thing at the same time gave me some comfort that perhaps I wasn't going crazy, and maybe we just really weren't supposed to go down that road.

On a different occasion, we were knocking on doors in a group of four apartment towers. With four apartments per floor, ten floors, and four towers, we were trying to knock on a total of 160 doors during that tracting session. We went through the first three towers without a single person being interested in hearing our message. We started at the tenth floor of the fourth tower and began working our way down. We got to the third floor and knocked on a door, and a gruff, middle-aged man answered the door. We introduced ourselves and asked him if he'd be interested in talking about the gospel. He abruptly came out of his apartment and started physically shoving us while yelling Hungarian obscenities at us. He continued chasing us and yelling at us, while adding an occasional shove, until we made it to the first floor and exited the building. We crossed the street to get away from the man, who continued yelling at us as he stood at the tower entrance. After taking a few minutes to regain our composure, I turned to my trainer.

"If my mission is going to be two years of this, then I'm not sure I want to stay here," I confided in him.

"Let's head home and call it a night, and you can give it some more thought once we get home," he responded.

Once we got home, I told my trainer that I needed some time alone to think. He went into a separate room, and a couple days later told me that he was praying for me during that time. I sat in the chair and tried to emotionally mend myself from the tough experience I had just endured. I started casually leafing through the pages of my scriptures, but nothing seemed to be relevant to my current situation or give me any comfort. It was in that moment that the words, "Read your patriarchal blessing," entered my mind. I found the travel copy of my blessing, reduced in size and laminated, and started to carefully read it, and I came to the section regarding my mission. The blessing talked about how I would faithfully serve a full-time mission, and how I would hate to leave the mission when it was time for me to return home. The blessing's foretelling of my completed, successful mission gave me the courage to emotionally heal that evening and to not give up on the mission, regardless of any obstacles that would come my way.

12

FIERY SPIRITS

Budapest District X

After 5 months in Szombathely, the mission president moved me to District X in Budapest. Most of our missionary work in this location was in the Pest side of Budapest, which is east of the Danube River, with the Buda side taking up the west bank. Pest is characterized by flatter terrain, lower incomes, and modest residences, while the Buda side has more hilly terrain, higher incomes, and fancier homes. Generally speaking, Budapest is definitely more modern and westernized than the more rural towns in Hungary, but it still has a dirtier and more dilapidated feel than cities such as Zürich, Switzerland, for example.

Members of the Church of Jesus Christ of Latter-Day Saints believe in modern day scripture that is in addition to the Old and New Testaments of the Bible. These additional scriptures include the Book of Mormon, the Doctrine & Covenants, and the Pearl of Great Price. I was reading the Doctrine & Covenants one evening after a long day of missionary work in this area, when I suddenly felt the Holy Spirit whisper to me that Joseph Smith was a true prophet of God. Along with this whisper came a powerful warm feeling that flooded through my body. This strong witness strengthened my testimony of the truthfulness of the Church and its message.

My first companion in this area was a tall ginger from Orem, UT. He was an excellent organist and chess player. Before his mission, while he was still a teenager, he started his own computer business. He would buy computer parts separately, assemble the computers himself, and then sell the computers for more than he paid for the parts. However, as a missionary he didn't work very hard, and we didn't get along very well during our time together.

Once he was transferred to a different city, there were two missionaries that replaced him, such that my new companionship had three missionaries in it. One of the new missionaries was a short blonde guy from Utah, and the other was a dark-haired, stocky guy from South Carolina. Both of them were quite good looking, which caused us problems from time to time with aggressive Hungarian girls. A good example of this occurred while we were knocking on doors and were invited inside by a kind older lady. She took us to her backyard and asked for our help with some manual labor items. The sun was hot that day and the three of us were sweating profusely as we moved some heavy items and chopped some wood for her. My two companions decided to take their shirts off because of the heat and sweat, but I decided to leave mine on, thinking it inappropriate for a missionary to be bare-chested in front of women. Shortly after that a few Hungarian girls our age emerged from the house. The old lady called out to us in Hungarian, saying, "Why don't you take a break from that and come have some lunch with me and my granddaughters?" She had a shaded canopy set up in her backyard to protect us from the sun, and we all sat at a rickety, wooden picnic table under the canopy. The girls had already positioned themselves at the table, making it impossible for the three of us missionaries to sit together, forcing us to each sit by one of the girls. We didn't want to make a scene and ask the girls to move, so each of us took a seat next to one of the girls. The grandma started serving us delicious Hungarian food and we all started eating while engaging in small talk with the older lady. The girls were very quiet but unusually attentive to the missionaries. The girl sitting next to me had short blonde hair, light blue eyes, and pale skin. She was wearing a white blouse and a very short skirt. Without saying a word, she looked directly and deeply into my eyes, with a slight, peaceful smile on her lips, and then placed her left hand high up on my right thigh with a gentle squeeze. In that moment I started to see that they were not interested in the religious message we had to share, and I realized that the Hungarian grandma was trying to set us up with her granddaughters. We quickly finished the meal and bid them farewell, aiming for a hasty exit without offending them. The grandma asked us when we would return, and we told her we'd be in touch.

On another occasion the three of us went to visit a member of the congregation who was a goat farmer. As we arrived at his house, we noticed a large male goat tethered to the front fence, lazily grazing on the front lawn. The farmer came out of his house before we even got to the front door and warmly greeted us. He immediately brought us to his backyard to give us a tour of his goat farming operation. The backyard was partitioned with rudimentary metal fencing, housing three adult female goats and a larger number of baby goats. He referred to the adult male goat in front of his house as his 'lawnmower', considering the large quantities of grass the goat would consume. After the brief tour, he brought us inside and we all sat down.

"So, how exactly does this goat farming thing work?" I asked him in Hungarian.

"Well, I use the females for their milk. Also, the male goat out front mates with the females, which is why you saw so many younger goats in the backyard. Then I use the younger goats for their meat," he responded. "I use as much of the goat milk and meat for myself as I can, and what I can't use myself, I sell to neighbors and in the market in town. I'm actually glad you all came here today, because I need help slaughtering one of the younger goats. I usually get my neighbors to help me, but they've been sick lately, and I can't do it on my own," he continued.

The three of us missionaries sat there dumbfounded until the farmer broke the silence.

"Here, let's say a prayer for the young goat before we slaughter him. I'll offer the prayer," he said.

The farmer prayed, giving thanks for the goat and for the meat it would provide, and asking that the goat wouldn't feel pain as we slaughtered it. Praying over an animal we were about to slaughter was a new experience for me. The farmer closed the prayer and led us to the backyard for the next new experience: the slaughter itself. None of the three of us missionaries had ever slaughtered an animal before, and the farmer noticed our apprehension and fear.

"Have any of you slaughtered an animal before?" he asked.

We all shook our heads, and the farmer let out an audible sigh. He then proceeded to give us instructions.

"I'll need two of you to help with this," he started. We all looked at each other and engaged in some short negotiations as we all wanted to avoid doing it, until we decided that the short blonde from Utah would be the one to not participate.

"Okay," the farmer continued, pointing to my companion from South Carolina. "You will grab his hind legs, holding one leg in each hand." Then he turned to me, "You will grab his short horns there, one in each hand. Then, when I tell you to, both of you lift the goat up so that his front legs are no longer touching the ground, and then I will slit his throat with this knife. He'll move around and make noise, so you'll need to hold him as firmly as you can while the blood drains into this basin here."

A few moments later, we proceeded as he instructed. Our companion that wasn't participating was watching as we started. However, once the farmer slit the goat's throat, blood started pouring out, and the goat started bleating during its death throes. It became too much for our blonde companion to handle. He grimaced, plugged his ears, closed his eyes, and turned around for the remainder of the process. After the bleeding and bleating had both subsided, the farmer turned to us and said, "Good job, elders. Please head inside and I'll be in shortly to join you." We headed into his kitchen, which had a window view of where the farmer continued processing the goat. He hung the goat by his hind legs on a tall wooden frame and started quickly skinning him as we looked away in disgust. As we all processed what had just happened, he joined us a few minutes later in the kitchen. "Thank you for your help today, elders. I really appreciate it. Before you leave, please have some chocolate milk," he offered. Looking for anything to get our minds off of what we had just experienced, we all quickly and eagerly accepted his offer. He poured some milk from his fridge into three cups, mixed some chocolate powder into it, and then served us. As soon as I took a drink, I had some sort of an involuntary hiccup that almost caused me to spew the chocolate milk through my nose. I had never had goat milk before, and I started suspecting that's what he used to make the chocolate milk. "This chocolate milk tastes a bit funny. Are you sure the milk you used is okay?" I asked. "It's perfectly fine. I just milked my female goats this morning, so it's actually quite fresh!" he replied. I forced down the rest of the chocolate goat milk in one gulp, not wanting to appear ungrateful or impolite, and we left shortly thereafter.

On a separate occasion, a group of missionaries in the area decided to go to a nice Chinese restaurant, and it had been quite a while since I had some good Chinese food. As we all sat down, a Chinese waiter showed up. It was a bit of a spectacle having a Chinese person speaking Hungarian to American missionaries, but we were eventually able to understand him through his accent.

"Would you all like to have some tea?" he asked. At this point it's important for me to remind the reader that members of the LDS church are not supposed to consume non-herbal tea or alcoholic drinks.

"We can only drink the tea if it's herbal tea," one of the missionaries in our group responded.

"Oh, it's herbal tea," the waiter quickly responded. "I'll bring some out for all of you, but you don't have to drink it if you don't want to," he explained. Shortly later, he brought out small cups of tea to each missionary and started taking food orders.

I reached out to the small cup of tea and took a sip. I had consumed a small variety of alcoholic drinks prior to my mission and could immediately tell that the tea had alcohol in it. I set the cup down and immediately warned the rest of the missionaries, many of whom were already taking their first sip as well.

"Don't drink the tea, it has alcohol in it," I softly mentioned to them, while trying to not make a scene in the restaurant.

The variety of responses that ensued was very reflective of the different types of personalities that go on a mission. One missionary responded with a sly smile on his face, "Tastes fine to me!" as he raised the cup to take a second drink. Another exclaimed, "So THAT's what alcohol tastes like!" The most epic response was when one of the missionaries buried his face in his hands while shaking his head, and started crying. "Alcohol has never touched my lips, and now I've broken the Word of Wisdom!" he stated dramatically. The Word of Wisdom is the modern-day scripture that prohibits members of the LDS church from consuming alcohol, tobacco, and other addictive substances. Later when we were back at one of the missionary apartments, the distraught missionary picked up the phone, put it on speaker, and called the mission president, who is typically an older, retired gentleman. As soon as the mission president answered the phone, the missionary started crying again about how he had never had alcohol before and how bad he felt about breaking the rules and so forth. After the missionary finally took a breath, the mission president responded, "Don't you have any work to do, elder? Get back to work!" With that the mission president hung up the phone, and we all stood in amazement and confusion, and some of us even laughed as we processed the mission president's unexpected and unsympathetic response.

<u>Miskolc</u>

While it was still summertime in 1998, I was transferred to a country town called Miskolc (pronounced MEESH-colts). The town was full of spiritually-frustrated residents. Most of the town's inhabitants were Catholic, but the local priest had lost their trust after it was exposed that he was granting forgiveness of sins in exchange for sexual favors from the young women in the congregation. When sharing the message of our church, it was common for us to hear the response of "I'm Catholic, but I hate the priests." Gaining the trust of the people in this area was difficult because of this bad experience they had with religion.

A missionary in a different companionship in this city was related to a prominent youth speaker in our church and had a lot of good ideas for moving the missionary work forward in the area. He recommended a book to us called 'Teaching with Spiritual Power' by Jerry Wilson. He had a copy of the book, and we all took turns reading it. One of the main premises of the book was that a thorough understanding of the scriptures was required before one could be an effective teacher of the Gospel. In order to facilitate this deeper understanding of the scriptures, the author devised an elaborate system whereby the reader could use different colored pencils and shorthand notation in order to make scripture study more effective. After reading the book, I was excited to try this new approach to reading the scriptures. However, after we had all read the book and discussed it, my companion made a comment to the group of missionaries that I'll never forget. "You could spend your entire life locked away in a room just becoming the world's foremost scriptorian and theologian," he said. "However, my dad taught me that it was always better to just get out of the house and serve other people." As I thought about his words, they resonated strongly with me, and I realized that his comments were probably more in line with how Christ himself conducted his own ministry.

It was relatively hot and humid during the summer in this town. On days where we were outside for most of the day knocking on doors, it was common for my dark-colored slacks to have white crusty sweat stains on them from how much I was sweating during the day. In spite of the rough weather, I was hitting my groove as a missionary, finding more effective ways to do the work, and tapping into a deep well of energy allowing me to work hard every day. It was around this time that my companion was transferred to a different city and I received my first trainee missionary, where I was his first companion in the mission. He was a short Finnish guy from Utah, and he was most definitely not ready for the level of energy I was bringing on a daily basis. It perhaps came as a blessing in disguise for him when I fell tremendously ill, requiring me to stay home for several days. I tried to be effective working from home, making phone calls, setting up meetings, etc., but in the end, I could tell that I needed to get healthy again and get back out of the house. My 6'2" frame had gotten down to 155 lbs due to all the weight I had lost. One of the people we had been discussing the church with before I got ill found out about my situation. He stopped by the house and asked me in great detail about my symptoms. "I'm going to make you a special soup that will help you overcome this sickness," he said confidently in Hungarian. I was doubtful he would be able to help, due to the severity of the sickness. He came back later that evening with a small pot of soup.

"I want you to eat this entire pot of soup tonight, including all the greens," he instructed.

"What's in it?" I asked out of curiosity.

"You don't need to know about all the ingredients, but the carrot tops are the main one that's going to get you over this sickness," he replied.

I had never considered carrot tops to be a miracle healing drug, but I decided to do as he suggested. Over the course of a couple hours that evening I ate the entire small pot of soup and fell into a deep sleep shortly thereafter. My companion let me sleep in the next morning, and when I woke up, I literally felt none of the symptoms that had plagued me for so many days. His magic carrot top soup had somehow worked!

We didn't have a dedicated building for church meetings in this town, but the mission president had found a classroom in a girls' college dormitory where we held our Sunday meetings. The only way into our meeting area was to walk down the hall past numerous college girl dorm rooms. The dorms were set up such that there was one bathroom that served a large number of dorm rooms, so it was not uncommon for us to encounter girls wrapped in towels heading to and from the showers on our way to church. The local Hungarian church members didn't think much of this dynamic, but it was a bit unnerving for us young, male missionaries trying not to think about girls for two years.

The woman that translated the Book of Mormon from English to Hungarian was also in this congregation. She was a native Hungarian, but her English was just perfect. We asked her how she got so good at English that she was asked to do the translation. It turned out that when she was a young woman, she worked as a nanny for a wealthy family in California for a number of years, and her English skills really started to shine. After she finished the Book of Mormon translation, she then participated in translating the church hymns from English to Hungarian as well.

We made some inroads with the local youth and managed to get some of them interested in the church as well. One of our most popular and effective ways of connecting with them was a weekly soccer game between the local missionaries and the Hungarian youth in the town. The event was always well attended and everybody had fun. At times it would become quite competitive, as both missionaries and Hungarian youth would jostle each other as they jockeyed for position in the game. One of the youth was a 6'2", 16-year-old girl with pale skin and long dark brown hair. During one game, she was on the opposing team and the two of us were fighting for control of the ball. Without thinking what

173

I was doing, I moved my legs quickly to try to snatch the ball and swung out my right arm inadvertently in the process. My hand landed squarely on one of her breasts and remained there longer than either of us expected. Both of us stopped in our tracks, while somebody took control of the ball and the other players continued to play while we stood there awkwardly.

"I'm so sorry!" I quickly blurted out in Hungarian. She just stood there blushing, saying nothing for a moment. Then she finally broke her silence and with a curious tone in her voice, said, "It's okay...it was an accident, right?" A question like that would typically be considered rhetorical in an American conversation. However, with the tone of her voice and her body language, it almost seemed as if she actually wanted an answer as to whether I intended to do it or not. I thought my apology would have conveyed that it was an accident. Years later this same girl ended up marrying a missionary from Utah. After they got married, I asked her how she knew he was the one for her. Hungary has a national celebration on August 20th where they commemorate the formation of the country over 1,000 years ago. She had been hanging out with a few missionaries during this celebration, and one of them had grabbed her butt during the festivities. "That was when I knew he was the one for me," she told me. I realized that Hungarian women appreciated confident or even more aggressive men, and it made her response to our awkward encounter years earlier more understandable. I already knew that I was fairly naïve and inexperienced as a young man, but this made me realize even more deeply that I still had a lot to learn about women.

Újpest

After several months in Miskolc, I was transferred to Újpest (pronounced OO-ee-pesht), which is in the northeastern corner of the Budapest metropolitan area. I was made a district leader in this area. The various missionary leadership positions include assistant to the president, district leader, zone leader, and branch president. I served as an assistant to the president during my two months in the missionary training center. As a district leader, I was expected to oversee a group of 12 missionaries. The Újpest area was full of older people that had strong, negative memories of the communism that was forced upon them by the Russian occupation. Older women would tell us about how they were forced to get abortions so that they could remain in the workforce. Others would talk about how they couldn't practice their own religion, but rather had to either engage in the state-sponsored religion or do nothing. Still others recounted the fear of having communist agents in trenchcoats and red ties show up at their door. Indeed, just having missionaries show up in similar attire triggered PTSD-type flashbacks in some of the older Hungarian generation. It was of course not helpful for our missionary work to have people thinking that we had any association whatsoever with the Russian occupation, so some of us would avoid wearing red ties for that very reason.

When the Russian soldiers started leaving Hungary in 1990, the country transitioned from a communist regime to a socialist structure. Many of the Hungarian leaders under the communist regime slipped into leadership roles in the new socialist platform, causing many Hungarians to believe that socialism was just communism in sheep's clothing. The country started engaging in democracy-related activities as well, but some people struggled under the new structure. One man explained to us, "Of all the atrocities we endured under communism, at least I had bread on the table." Many Hungarians were ill-equipped to deal with the new democratic system, where being poor meant you might not actually be able to get food, which, according to the tales we heard, was not something most people had to worry about under the communist regime.

I particularly remember one elderly lady that converted to the church while I was serving in the Újpest area. After her baptism, we came across another elderly lady who had a strong interest in the church. We thought the recently converted woman might be able to share her conversion experience with the new investigator. We brought the new convert to one of our visits in the investigator's home, and they seemed to form an instant connection. They started quickly and happily conversing with each other in Hungarian while my companion and I just watched. Before us sat two older women, probably both in their eighties, talking about the Gospel of Jesus Christ. While we looked on, I had what I can only describe as some sort of a spiritual vision. Without closing my eyes, it seemed that everything around me turned into shades of gray, while the two older women became young, strong, fiery spiritual beings, in colors of yellow, orange, and red, and they burned brightly and fiercely as they conversed with each other. This lasted only a few short moments, after which my vision returned to normal and I saw only the two old, wrinkled ladies sitting before me in their mortal, earthly forms. I pondered the experience in my mind for weeks after it happened. I realized that our spirits radiate an energy that may be stronger than our physical appearance would sometimes suggest. I considered the spiritual experience to be a special manifestation of the Old Testament scripture in 1 Samuel 16:7, which states, "Look not on his countenance, or on the height of his stature…for the Lord seeth not as man seeth; for man looketh on the outward appearance, but the Lord looketh on the heart."

13

THE DEATH PROPHECY

For my final area I was transferred to a city called Érd (pronounced AIRED), which lies just outside of the southwestern corner of Budapest. I was moved there by the mission president in order to take over a zone leader position which was being vacated by a missionary that was returning home. Zone leaders are typically in charge of a handful of districts, putting them in charge of a large number of missionaries and a large geographical area. I was given a car in this role to make travel more efficient. I had a large number of spiritual experiences in this final area, some of which I will highlight here.

The zone leader I was replacing was considered one of the humblest missionaries in the country and had an unusually strong connection to the Spirit. He was teaching an investigator by the name of Rita, who was a healthy 26-year-old woman living in Százhalombatta (pronounced SAZ-HALL-ohm-BAH-tah), which is a town just south of Érd. She asked him to give her a priesthood blessing before he returned home to America, not because she was ill (she seemed healthy at that point), but because she was seeking spiritual counsel. To everyone's surprise in the room, in the blessing he told her that she was going to die soon. Immediately after he finished giving her the blessing, he was at a complete loss of words regarding the seeming death sentence he had just pronounced on her. Fast forward a bit, after the zone leader I had replaced had returned to America, my companion and I continued meeting with Rita, who was always cheerful and enjoyed our discussions. One day we went to her apartment to chat, and we noticed the door to her apartment was already open. We let ourselves in and encountered her boyfriend, crying on her bed, surrounded by a few policemen. "Rita died," the boyfriend said somberly. We spoke with the policemen to try to determine the cause of death. All they could tell us at the time was that it was not a suicide. After the shock of her death wore off, I remembered the blessing that the missionary had given her, warning her of her impending death. We never found out the exact cause of death, but the former zone leader's prediction of her death was very eerie.

It is common for investigators, as they try to get to know the missionaries better, to ask them what they want to do once they return home after the mission. Most missionaries talk about college, sports, and career intentions when the conversation comes to this. However, my first companion in Érd always had the same reply, as he would tell them, "I'm going to be a rock star." The people he would tell that to would have a variety of responses, ranging from "good luck with that" to more positive responses regarding the beauty of following one's dreams. He had a guitar and was quite gifted musically. He was from the Orange County, CA, area and was very serious about his musical ambitions. Sometimes he spent time playing guitar when he was supposed to be engaged in missionary work, so his music became a point of contention between us from time to time. However, after he returned from his mission, he defied all the naysayers and has been touring the world as the drummer in a wildly popular deathcore band for the past 16 years.

Some of the people we would encounter would confuse us with the Amish. This was a result of a movie called Witness, which came out in 1985 and highlighted the Amish community. The Hungarian translators accidentally translated 'Amish' as 'Mormon', so those that had seen the movie were frequently confused by the difference between the two religions. One guy we met on the street, near where my car was parked, said, "Yeah, I know all about your church. You guys are the ones that don't believe in cars and electricity."

"Not true," I replied. "That's the Amish. That's my car right there, and our meetinghouse up in that building there has plenty of electricity!"

Four of us missionaries all lived together in the same house, and one of the four was a former junior state wrestling champion in Arizona. Having a tall and sturdy frame, I foolishly thought that I could give him a run for his money. "Let's have a go then," I told him playfully one day as we were at home messing around. I thought that my height and strength advantage would win out at the end. However, his wrestling technique was exceptional, and he had me fully pinned in less than three seconds.

A branch president is the head of a congregation in a country where the church is less developed. The branch president in Érd was a native Hungarian at the time, but he asked to be released from his calling for personal reasons. Without a suitable Hungarian native alternate, the mission president asked me to assume the role of branch president in addition to my zone leader duties. For the last 3 months of the mission, I was both a zone leader, leading a large number of missionaries in a large geographical area, and a branch president, leading a congregation of over a hundred native Hungarians and presiding over church services on Sunday. These two leadership positions demanded a lot of my time, but I also made sure to spend time doing 'normal' missionary work as well.

As part of my role as zone leader, I had to establish numeric goals on a variety of metrics for the missionaries in my zone to try to achieve. These metrics included number of people investigating the church, hours spent per week engaged in missionary work, hours spent engaged in community service activities, number of baptisms, etc. It came to my attention that a number of the missionaries in my zone thought the goals I set were too difficult to achieve. In spite of the demanding nature of my two leadership callings, I decided with the support of my companion that we were going to do a week where my companion and I achieved every single numeric target, just to show the zone that the goals were achievable. At one point that week I quite literally collapsed from exhaustion while we were home one afternoon, but at the end of the week, we had met every single target that I had established. The murmuring from missionaries subsided after that.

As a new branch president, I had to select two counselors to support me in the calling. I asked my missionary companion to serve as one of my counselors, and he happily obliged. For the other spot, after praying about it I felt strongly that a particular man in our congregation was supposed to fill the role. The only problem was that he owned a chain of wineries across the country, which had made him a very wealthy man. Before he joined the LDS church, he would sample the wine before distributing it to all of his stores. However, after he joined the LDS church, he would still sample the wine to make sure it tasted right, but then he would spit it out instead of swallowing it. He had looked into selling the whole empire in order to get out of the alcohol business, but to make a long story short, that option was not looking promising. I made my intention known to the congregation that he would fill the remaining seat as one of my counselors. One of the more respected members of the congregation, who was considered one of the top violinists in the country, approached me after that Sunday's services.

"Do you know what this man does for his work?" he stated incredulously. "He works with wine all day. A man like that, who works in an industry that's against the Word of Wisdom, should not be in a leadership position in our branch."

He was so forceful with his reservations about this man that I told him I would check with the mission president for guidance. I called the mission president and explained the situation to him, and he told me it was a tricky one. He told me that he would contact the regional church authority in charge of overseeing the entire eastern European area and get back to me. The mission president later told me how their conversation went.

"Did the branch president pray about this man serving as his counselor and feel that he was the right one for the position?" the regional authority asked. The mission president replied that I had. "Does the prospective counselor follow the Word of Wisdom?" the regional authority then asked. The mission president replied in the affirmative on that one as well. "Well then," the regional authority responded, "I don't see what the problem is." With that simple confirmation, I was able to proceed in calling the man to be my other counselor, and he served well in the position.

One morning while I was studying my scriptures and praying before leaving the house for the day's work, I prayed and inquired if there was anything in particular that Heavenly Father wanted me to do that day, instead of what we were already planning. I received a strong response that Heavenly Father wanted my companion and me to go to a town called Törökbálint, which lies just north of Érd, and that we were to "flood the area with the Book of Mormon." I was also told, through the Spirit, that "by doing so you will be planting seeds of faith, the fruits of which you will not harvest yourselves." As a missionary I was so used to trying to get my foot in the door so that we could have Gospel discussions with investigators and help them progress towards baptism. However, with this prompting, I felt that we were just supposed to place Books of Mormon in as many hands as possible in Törökbálint. We were giving so many books away that we had to drive to the mission president's home to get additional boxes full of Books of Mormon. It became apparent that even people that weren't interested in having a

Gospel discussion were still interested in receiving a free book and putting it on their bookshelf. I'm sure that in the 23 years that have passed since then that some of those Books of Mormon eventually got picked up and read, and may have even brought some people closer to Christ in the process.

One day while my companion and I were knocking on doors, we were approached by the city police. They stopped us as we were heading to the next house.

"You can't knock on doors like this anymore. We have received complaints from some residents about two men walking from house to house," they said calmly but firmly in Hungarian.

"This is an important aspect of our missionary work," I replied. "If we don't knock on doors, how are we supposed to talk with people about our church?"

"Can't you just leave a flyer in their mailbox? Then they can contact you if they're interested," they replied.

"People typically don't respond if you just leave a flyer. We have more success if we're able to engage them in person and have a brief conversation about their interest," I continued.

"Well, we've told you to stop, so you need to stop," they demanded.

We headed home feeling a bit defeated. Once we arrived back at the house, we found the other two missionaries there as well.

"The cops told us to stop tracting," one of them quickly told me.

"Yeah, I know. They just told us the same thing," I responded.

After strategizing together for a bit with the other missionaries, I started to feel emboldened that I needed to find a solution on my own, rather than bringing the problem to the mission president, who already had enough on his plate. I turned to my companion and said, "Let's go, we're gonna fix this."

We drove straight over to police headquarters for the city. I walked right in and said, "I'd like to speak with the chief of police." Seeing us in our missionary formal attire with our badges, and with my firm and frustrated tone, the policeman at the front desk decided not to mess with me, as he headed back to get his superior. Another man emerged from behind the front desk and said, "Can I help you?" I explained how some of his policemen had stopped us from tracting, and started explaining to him why we needed to be able to continue that practice. "This decision was made by the mayor, so if you have an issue with it, you'll need to take it up with her," he replied.

We headed directly over to the city headquarters and walked into the main office. I approached the lady at the front desk, introduced myself and my companion, and said, "I'd like to speak with the mayor."

"Do you have an appointment?" she inquired.

"No, but it's urgent and very important that we talk with her," I replied.

"One moment," she said, as she called up to the mayor's office. A few moments later, she said, "The mayor will see you now, please head up those stairs behind me."

We headed up the stairs, entered the mayor's office, and then sat down after exchanging a few pleasantries.

"What can I do for you?" she asked politely.

I recounted the day's events for her, and she proceeded to state the same things the first policeman had stated in getting us to stop tracting. She said she didn't want the people in her city to be annoyed by missionaries knocking on doors. I could tell that explaining to her why we needed to keep doing it wasn't changing her mind, and out of nowhere I surprised even myself with a spontaneous powerplay. The prime minister of Hungary at the time was a man by the name of Viktor Orbán. Even prior to Orbán's administration, the missionaries had been allowed to proselyte in Hungary for close to a decade. Thinking quickly on my feet, I changed my tone to be sterner and said, "Prime Minister Orbán knows that we're here, and our missionary work across the entire country is sanctioned by him. If you have a problem with us conducting our missionary work, then you need to take it up with Prime Minister Orbán. Otherwise, we will continue our work as usual." As she sat stunned by my forceful assertion, we thanked her for her time, turned around and quickly left.

Years later while pondering the experience, I wondered where the courage came from for me, only 21 years old at the time, to aggressively confront both the chief of police and the mayor of a city in a foreign country like that and win. The best explanation I could find for what might have happened can be found in Genesis 14:31 in the Joseph Smith Translation of the Old Testament, which refers to the Melchizedek Priesthood having the power to "subdue principalities and powers," if needed for the furthering of the Lord's work.

14

THE LONE PINE TAVERN

I finished the mission in Hungary one month too late in order to return to Dartmouth for the 1999 fall semester. This gave me a few months to relax before starting the college grind again. I was still not on great terms with my mother, so I decided to spend those few months with my aunt Nancy and her family in Orange, CA. The church officials in Orange County weren't aware of my return, so I had to hunt down the local Stake President in order to be released as a missionary. Once I took care of that business, I set out finding ways to keep myself busy for a few months. I decided against getting a job for those few months so that I could just relax and enjoy the break.

On days where I didn't have any plans, I spent time watching an unusual combination of MTV and C-SPAN, alternating between inappropriate music videos and ultra-dull government programming. Occasionally I would switch over and watch some tennis or some of the old VHS movies from my uncle Russ' collection. I also got heavily involved in family history research. At the time, a lot of the modern family history websites didn't exist yet, so the research involved a lot of family trees filled out on awkwardly-sized paper and visits to the local family history center. I also started jogging a bit on a regular basis to offset all the calories I was consuming in the form of Hot Pockets and microwave cheeseburgers.

In an effort to start adjusting to the college social scene again, I started attending two different institute groups. For the readers that are not LDS, institute is basically a class taught at the college level for LDS students, and serves as a springing board for a lot of group social activities for those same kids. I attended both the Costa Mesa and Cal State Fullerton institutes so that I could meet more LDS college students and start participating in their activities as well. I asked a girl at one of the institutes on a date to Knotts Berry Farm, a popular amusement park in the Orange County area. However, after accepting my invitation she stood me up, so I decided to go with one of my guy friends in the area instead. Another institute activity ended up being a hot tub activity, which was quite uncomfortable for me, since I had just spent two years avoiding women. While in the hot tub, I let out a little yelp and violently jerked my body away when a girl sitting next to me touched me with her leg. It was after that experience that I realized I had a long way to go in returning to normalcy with how I related to young women my age, now that the mission was over.

As I started regaining my confidence, I started going hot tubbing with my cousin and his friends. However, there was a bit of an age difference. I had just turned 21, while my cousin and his friends were all in their mid/late 20s. Now that I'm in my 40s, I don't see much difference between those two age categories, but at the time they seemed much more mature emotionally and socially to me. I started taking a liking to a tall, slender brunette that would frequently come to our nighttime hot tub festivities. We were all in the habit of being very open with our feelings, so it didn't take long for the whole group to learn that 21-year-old Jason had a thing for the 25-year-old brunette. One evening when the subject came up, my cousin decided to issue a warning to me in front of the entire group.

"Dude, she is very aggressive. You don't know what you're getting yourself into. If you pursue her, she will go for it, but you will have a hard time escaping."

While he was talking about her in the third person, she just continued sitting quietly in the hot tub, looking at me with a mischievous smile on her face and not denying anything my cousin had just said about her. After giving it some thought, I came to the conclusion that she would be a bit much for me at that point in my life, so I reluctantly passed on the opportunity.

My grandma down in San Diego wanted to see me and also said she had some construction projects for me to work on, so I decided to take the train down there and spend a few weeks with her. She had plenty of money to spend on the construction projects, so I ended up using redwood and oak for all the projects, even though it would have been much more affordable to use pine or something similar. The projects consisted of shoring up the awning supports in the back patio area, replacing the wood framing surrounding the wall separating the back

THE LONE PINE TAVERN

patio from the backyard, replacing some of the deck boards on her bedroom deck near the front of the house, and then building a set of stairs from the backyard to an elevated planter area where she had a number of flower bushes planted. I had the skills to perform all these projects myself after my experience as a carpenter's helper the summer before my mission in Hungary. My deceased grandfather's tools were all still in his garage, so I was able to get going with all the projects without delay.

It was while I was working on the stairs in the backyard that my grandma decided to order me a pizza to enjoy once I was done. When the pizza arrived, she stepped out onto the back patio.

"Jason, your pizza is here!" she yelled over to me.

"Thanks, grandma," I responded. "I'm almost done with this part I'm working on, then I'll call it a day and come in."

She nodded in agreement and headed back inside. The part I was trying to finish ended up being a bit stubborn, keeping me out there longer than I had anticipated. A short while later, I heard the sound of sirens approaching. I looked up and wiped the sweat from my brow, and then I suddenly noticed there was black smoke billowing out from the front of the house. As I stood up and started panicking, a neighbor rushed over and explained that he was the one that called the fire department, and the fire truck arrived shortly thereafter. They quickly put out the fire with minimal damage done to the house, and after a while the firemen and the neighbor left. I headed into the kitchen and noticed that the oven was a complete, blackened mess.

"Grandma, what happened in here?" I asked her.

"Well, when your pizza came but you didn't want to come in yet, I decided to turn the oven on and put the pizza box in there, in order to keep it warm for you!" she responded. "But then I forgot that I had put it in there, and it must have caught fire."

At this juncture I should point out that my paternal grandmother was not the type to make these kinds of mistakes. She was Phi Beta Kappa at the University of Utah and prided herself in her exceptional intelligence. When this lapse of judgment occurred, we started worrying that there might be a larger problem looming. My father's side of the family had always agreed that nobody would put grandma in a nursing home. However, once the signs of dementia started settling in, the family had a difficult decision to make. As the years went on, after I had already returned to college, my aunt Nancy and my cousin Nikki started taking care of grandma. However, as the dementia continued to worsen and ultimately progress into full Alzheimer's, she became more of a danger to herself and those around her, and taking care of her started taking a toll on my aunt's health as well. It was at that point that the family decided to go against their prior agreement and put grandma in a nursing home.

Returning to my time with my grandma that fall, I also found time to go to the San Diego LDS temple, which is located in La Jolla, CA. Local residents refer to it as 'The Castle', due to its elaborate and ornamental architecture. It was while I was in the temple there one day that one of the elderly temple workers walked over to me and started talking with me. I told him that I had recently returned from my mission and was staying with family until I returned to college in January. He quickly moved our conversation towards dating and asked if I was looking for that special someone.

"That would be great if I met someone," I responded, "but I'm only here in Southern California for a few months before I return to college, so I'm not expecting to meet anyone before then."

"Don't worry about how the girl looks when you're dating. She will become more beautiful to you over time as your love grows."

I felt like he had just shared something special with me, but I wasn't sure if it would apply to me or not. I thanked him kindly for the advice and left shortly thereafter. I then returned to Orange County, made my final preparations, and headed back to Dartmouth.

The years of 1997 to 1999, while I was on my mission in Hungary, were also a time of rapid innovation in technology. Email was a new thing for college students in the mid-90s but had become much more widespread by the time I returned to the States. As I returned to campus, I started adjusting not only to college life again, but also to using new technology that had not been a part of my life as a missionary. I received an email from the institute teacher at Dartmouth welcoming the LDS students to the new semester. I chose to snoop the recipient list of the email and then look those students up in the 'face book' that the college issued each year. This 'face book' was in paperback format and simply had a headshot of each student and a short caption about where they were from. These types of 'face books' were in use at a few other colleges as well, and the one at Harvard was the precursor to the online/digital behemoth that we all know as Facebook today. Culturally, the men at Dartmouth would typically use the face book to scope out girls for potential dates. Like a typical guy, I can't deny that I ended up spending a little more time studying the pictures of the LDS girls than of the LDS guys as I looked up the other students in my institute class. While doing so I came across the profile of an unusually gorgeous girl with blonde hair by the name of Sarah Bradford. I quickly came to the conclusion that she was way out of my league and slowly closed the book.

My first chance to meet some of these other LDS students came soon after the new semester started. There was a small bar called the Lone Pine Tavern located in the Collis building, which was considered a hub for student activities. One particular evening a band that included a couple of LDS students was playing live in the Lone Pine Tavern, so all the LDS students decided to attend in a show of support. As most of the other LDS students were on campus for the fall semester as well, I was one of only 2 or 3 new LDS students that didn't start back at the college until the winter semester. All the LDS students were seated at a rather long table, so I started going around, shaking hands, and introducing myself. Then out of the corner of my eye, I spotted the gorgeous blonde seated at the far corner of the table opposite from the spot where I was standing. In an overeager and awkward way, I leaned over the table with an outstretched hand towards her, rather than walking around to where she was seated, in an effort to introduce myself.

"Hi, I'm Jason," I yelled over the loud music, as I remained stretched out over the table. After what seemed like a brief hesitation on her part, during which she let out a chuckle and a smile at the spectacle before her, she extended her hand as well, responding with "I'm Sarah, nice to meet you."

The day soon came for our first institute class. Our institute teacher had a way with words and a love of the Gospel that made every meeting with her special. Our institute meetings were typically held on Wednesday evenings in one of the posh Baker library rooms. After our first institute meeting, I decided to ask a girl on a date. I didn't know any of the girls very well and had not spent any amount of time with them in order to develop romantic feelings for any of them, but I didn't want to let any of that prevent me from getting the dating process started. I figured the institute class president would be just as good as any to be my first date. To make it feel less targeted, I spoke with my friend and asked him if he'd like to ask a girl as well, and then we could do a double date. He agreed, and then to my surprise, he decided to ask Sarah to be his date.

We had a couple different things scheduled for the double date, including a concert and then milkshakes afterwards. I felt bad because my date was trying to engage in conversation with me, but I felt drawn to Sarah and couldn't help but focus on her for the entire evening. I was a bad date that evening, and I knew it. After we had dropped the girls off, my friend and I started walking together towards our own dorms.

As we were walking, I turned to him and asked, "You don't really like Sarah, do you? I mean, if you do, I respect that, and I wouldn't want to get in the way."

As I stumbled over my words, he could clearly see that I had feelings for her. "Nah, man! Go for it!" he responded, with a smile on his face. A wave of relief came over me, and I felt like I had the green light to start to get to know Sarah better.

Without wasting any more time with any of the other girls, I decided to ask Sarah on a date. She accepted. Before the day came for our first date, I decided to ask her on another, separate date. Clearly not reading the rule book on not coming across as overeager, I was just focused on finding ways to spend more time with her. She accepted the second date as well, although she didn't let me off the hook without poking a little fun at me for my excessive enthusiasm. As we started spending more time together, I noticed that I was really enjoying our dates and getting to know her better. However, all of those feelings seemed to take an abrupt, unexpected turn one day.

The Phoenix Suns were going to play the Boston Celtics in Boston. The game seemed meaningful, as I spent a large portion of my childhood growing up in Phoenix, and Sarah had lived briefly in Boston and loved it. We decided we'd go to the game together and maybe even paint our faces to show our support for the two different teams. However, before the day came, Sarah received the news that her maternal grandmother that lived down in North Carolina had passed away. Sarah made plans to go be with family for the funeral, and we were of course unable to enjoy our NBA date in Boston.

When she returned, I realized that I needed to be a source of support for her. I started thinking of ways that I could emotionally support her during that difficult time, as she remained distraught for quite a while after she returned from the funeral. I was anxious and hopeful that we could return to the happiness we were enjoying before her grandmother passed, but it just seemed to not be bouncing back to that as quickly as I thought it would. As she continued to grieve, and my selfish thoughts of returning to the happy dating days persisted, I started feeling that maybe I was slowly being pushed into the 'friend zone'. I felt that I needed to do something to counteract that slide into the friend zone, but I was too shy to do it in person, so I decided to write a lengthy email to her in which I would share my true feelings for her. I felt like I was taking a big risk by making the first move in determining the relationship with her, and I felt butterflies in my stomach as I finished the email and pressed send. I figured that based on how sincere yet strong my email came across, that it would either end our relationship or put us on a different path. After what seemed like an eternity, she responded positively to my email, giving me confidence that our relationship could progress into more romantic territory. Not too long after that email exchange, we shared our first kiss on Leap Day, February 29th, 2000, in her room in the North dorm building. After I left her dorm room that evening and headed back to my room, I looked up to admire the bright waning crescent moon in the night sky and felt a deep happiness and excitement for the future.

Now that I felt we were headed into more exclusive territory in our dating relationship, I jealously decided it was time to scare off a couple other suitors. One of them was a young man who was also a student at Dartmouth. The other was a good-looking young man back in Utah who was a 'hometown honey' of sorts for Sarah. When I was over at Sarah's dorm, I noticed she had a picture of the Utah guy on her small dorm room fridge, so I figured she must still have some feelings for him, although they didn't seem to be in frequent contact. The Dartmouth young man, on the other hand, was in frequent contact with Sarah and was posing as the ultra-supportive friend, although I could see through his act and could tell he had feelings for her. Over the course of a number of awkward and sometimes painful conversations, Sarah was able to put these other two young men behind her as we became more serious.

One of our favorite dates was to go to the music practice rooms, and I would just hang out in there and listen to Sarah play the piano. I felt my love for her grow as I would watch her play on a regular basis. We would also stay up late talking about countless topics. One time we were up late talking, and her roommates wanted to go to bed, so we moved our conversation to the dorm laundry room and talked until the sun came up the next morning. As we grew closer, we didn't feel the need to broadcast our relationship to the other LDS students at Dartmouth, so we continued dating somewhat in secret. However, signs of our affection for each other started slipping out in view of others. On one occasion as we were spending time together, we lost track of time and ended up being late to our institute class. We didn't think to stagger our late arrival, so when we showed up late together, there were more than a few raised eyebrows. One of our friends in common, a female hockey team member, sent an email to Sarah asking, "So, are you and Mr. Merrill a thing, or no?" At that point we realized the cat was probably out of the bag.

Sarah decided it was time for me to meet her mom and sisters in Baltimore. Her mom was working at Johns Hopkins University as a lung cancer research specialist at the time, and Sarah's sisters were both in high school. Sarah and I had talked about getting engaged prior to driving down to Baltimore, so this trip would also give me an opportunity to ask for Sarah's mother's permission or blessing to marry Sarah. I found an opportunity to talk with Sarah's mother about it after she returned home from work.

"I love your daughter very much and am thinking about asking her to marry me," I said as we sat in chairs across from each other in the kitchen. "I was hoping that you would give me your blessing to do so."

"You do not have my blessing," she responded. "She's too young, and I think you're ruining her life."

Her response was stern but not overly angry. It caught me off guard, as it hadn't occurred to me that she would respond so negatively. To make matters worse, after she refused to give me her blessing to marry her daughter, she kicked me out of her house.

"I don't want you sleeping in my house now that I know what you're trying to do. Take your bags with you when you leave," she demanded.

I knocked on the neighbor's door, and a middle-aged single man with a dark tan, medium height, and muscular build answered. After explaining my situation, he offered that I could sleep in his guest room.

The next morning after I woke up and showered, I headed back over to Sarah's mother's place. As she was preparing to leave for work, she approached the two of us and said, "I don't want you hanging around the house alone while I'm gone working. I'll drop you off at the mall and you can spend the day there while I'm working." In spite of her negativity, Sarah and I decided to make the most of our day at the mall and decided to go ring shopping. After finding a suitable engagement ring, we bought it that same day, and Sarah decided to wear it when her mom picked us up. Once she could tell that we were determined to get engaged, she eased up a little, but her negativity never fully subsided.

Back on campus, Sarah and I decided to make progress towards preparing for marriage. We took engagement pictures at a special garden near the Dartmouth campus. We chose November 11th, which just so happens to be Veteran's Day, to be the day we would get married. Sarah told me that it was important to her that we get married in the Mount Timpanogos LDS Temple in American Fork, UT, and I agreed. I started exercising more in an attempt to get in shape for marriage. On one such occasion, I was using a multi-hip machine in the Dartmouth gym. I had only ever seen girls use the machine, but that wasn't stopping me from using it. While I was going at it on that machine, Sarah's ex-boyfriend, who was a member of the Dartmouth football team, happened to be walking by with two of his thick-necked jock buddies. Upon seeing me he stopped in his tracks, started shaking his head with a look of disbelief and said, "Merrill, I don't know how you do it." I took it as an insult that he was wondering why Sarah would like a weird guy like me, but I ignored his comment and just kept exercising.

During the months before our marriage, I started renting a log cabin on a dirt road in Norwich, VT, and Sarah started a brain sciences internship at Mass General Hospital in Boston. She was slicing mice brains and conducting various types of stem cell research in her internship. We viewed the time apart towards the end of our engagement as a good thing. Our physical attraction to each other had been growing over the course of our engagement, but the LDS religion prohibits sex before marriage, and we had no intention of breaking that prohibition.

After our wedding ceremony in the Mount Timpanogos Temple, we had a lovely reception in the Utah County area, and then we headed up to Salt Lake City to stay at the Anniversary Inn for our wedding night. One of our wedding gifts, from an executive of the international boys' home organization that I lived at during my senior year of high school, was a week's worth of time share in the Bahamas for our honeymoon. However, once we got there, it was definitely not what we expected. We thought we'd be headed to one of those large, high-quality resorts, but this place was under heavy renovation and had more of a dingy, small motel feel. There was no food in the area we were in, so we ended up heading inland to try to find a supermarket where we could buy a few things. We quickly discovered that the inland part of the island had a very strong ghetto vibe and didn't seem very safe. Aside from typical honeymoon activities, we spent time playing cards, tennis, swimming and snorkeling in the clear blue ocean, and also lounging at a nearby water park. Eventually the honeymoon came to an end. We returned to our lives as undergraduate students at Dartmouth and started living together in the log cabin on a dirt road in Norwich, VT.

15

LANDING A SPACECRAFT ON MARS

In 2003 when I was working on my first of three master's degrees, I started applying for jobs at Lockheed Martin. It had always been a dream of mine to be involved in the engineering design of jet fighter planes, and Lockheed makes some of the best jet fighters in the world. However, when I started applying to engineering jobs on the Lockheed website, there were a few key factors that were working against me. Firstly, I didn't know at the time that Lockheed Martin receives over a million resumes per year globally, and the vast majority of these are submitted through their online system. Secondly, based on the geographical location of their main business units across the United States, Lockheed has a group of colleges that are considered 'target schools' for them, and

Dartmouth was not on this short list. Thirdly, I was new to the importance of the networking game and was about to learn a lesson about how powerful knowing the right people can be.

By mid 2004 I was finishing up my second master's degree and had started working full time for a couple of affiliated startup companies near Dartmouth. I had been applying to Lockheed jobs for over a year and had yet to receive a call back or an email showing interest in my candidacy. I completed my master's thesis in October and received feedback from the thesis committee chairman that my master's thesis was "of Ph.D. quality", which I took as high praise for all the work I put into it. However, on the heels of that success, shortly into the new year of 2005, the startup companies I was working for started struggling with their cash burn rate.

My manager brought me into his office and said, "We're going to have to start paying you with stock options instead of a paycheck."

"I can't pay my bills with stock options," I replied. I made it clear that stock option compensation was not going to work for me, as my financial situation as a fresh graduate with three young children at home was much different than that of my more experienced serial-entrepreneur colleagues. My manager was sensitive to my situation and decided to start paying me from his personal bank account.

While I deeply appreciated the financial sacrifice he was making to keep me paid, the whole situation motivated me to search even harder for a more stable work situation, as it was unclear to me how long my manager's support would extend. Shortly after this turn of events, I heard from a former classmate from my first master's program.

"Are you still interested in working at Lockheed?" he inquired via email.

"I am!" I enthusiastically replied. "I've been applying to jobs via their online system for a couple years now but have yet to score a single interview."

"Send me your resume," he wrote back. "One of my in-laws is related to the head of HR in the Space Systems division. I can make sure that the right person actually sees your resume."

Within two weeks I had three interview offers at Lockheed Martin.

The first opportunity would have been to work on the Fleet Ballistic Missile program. This would have been on the military side of the Space Systems division, and I would have had some involvement with our country's nuclear weapons program. However, the job was located in Sunnyvale, CA, and we realized this location would be too expensive for our family of 5, so we decided to not accept the interview for that one. My former classmate that helped me get the interviews later told me that if I had taken that position, I would have been on the same team as him.

The second opportunity was the realization of my childhood dream to work on jet fighters. The interview was at Lockheed's Fort Worth, TX, location in their aeronautics business unit. I showed up with a briefcase containing a copy of my 285-page long master's thesis. After brief introductions, I fished the thesis out of my briefcase and gently dropped it onto the interview table with a soft thud. The interviewer's eyes widened as she picked it up and started casually flipping through it. She put it back on the table and started describing the opportunity. I would be on the team responsible for the design and analysis of the wing on the F-35 stealth fighter. I had arrived at the interview in the mindset that my ability to get the job depended on my interview performance. However, at the conclusion of the interview, it became clear that I already had the job if I wanted it. I told them I would be in touch and headed back to New Hampshire, excited about the new opportunity.

The third opportunity was in the Civil Space division of the Space Systems business unit. This is the department involved in space exploration and is located primarily in Denver, CO. It was also the residence of the HR executive that was setting up all three opportunities for me. I finally got to meet him in person for the Denver interview, and he made it very clear to me that they wanted me working at Lockheed. Through the process of multiple interviews, they were just trying to find the right opportunity for me based on their needs and my interests. He took some time to discuss the various intriguing space exploration programs that had staffing needs. I returned to New Hampshire again with a lot on my mind.

Taking the stealth fighter job would have been the fulfillment of a childhood dream. However, I immediately fell in love with the Denver area after visiting for my interview, while I was very unimpressed with the Fort Worth landscape. The economics of the two different jobs were also slightly in favor of the Denver opportunity. After much discussion, Sarah and I decided to take the Denver opportunity. By March 2005, we had sold our condo in Lebanon, NH, and bought a home in Highlands Ranch, CO. We had left the world of entrepreneurship in favor of a steadier salary and world-class career opportunities in space exploration.

The first program I worked on was the Hubble Robotic Vehicle De-Orbit Module (HRVDM) program. The premise of that program was two-fold. Firstly, the Hubble Telescope required occasional repairs, and the only way to accomplish these repairs was for astronauts to perform a space shuttle mission, dock onto the telescope, and perform a spacewalk to manually perform the repairs. This approach to fixing the telescope was costly, and the associated extra-vehicular activity posed an added risk for the astronauts. This program proposed the construction of a robot that would be launched into space, dock onto the telescope, and perform all future necessary repairs on the telescope without the need for additional astronaut missions. The secondary goal of the program was to address the end-of-life scenario for the telescope. At some point the telescope would become inoperable and would need to be decommissioned. At that point, the telescope would join the ranks of other space trash orbiting the earth. The HRVDM robot would handle this by safely de-orbiting the telescope into the ocean once it reached the end of its life. I was hired into this program as a thermal analyst modeling heat transfer in space. Within the span of only a couple of weeks, I had started innovating a new way to analyze heat transfer in space assets and was later recognized with a Special Recognition Award for furthering the state-of-the-art in thermal analysis. Unfortunately, on the heels of this personal success, NASA decided to cancel the HRVDM program towards the end of April 2005. Having just moved my family across the country from New Hampshire to Colorado a month prior, I became very concerned about what the future would hold. However, I soon learned that once you're in the Lockheed family, they do everything they can to keep you at the company. One of the most notable examples of this was a military defense program at the Sunnyvale, CA, plant that employed over 1,000 people. The program was abruptly canceled one year, but due to the tremendous size of Lockheed and all of the various programs they run, all but 11 of those 1,000+ employees were absorbed into other Lockheed Martin programs and were saved from unemployment.

I applied to and was accepted into the Engineering Leadership Development Program, which accelerated my experience with different programs and teams. Within this leadership program, I was able to rotate through 6-month engagements with different programs and groups, including the Phoenix Mars Lander, the IT department, the Space Systems executive team, the Orion program, and Mission Operations.

On the Phoenix Mars Lander team, I was a thermal analyst responsible for modeling heat transfer in the spacecraft while it was traveling in space. While working on this program, I had the uncomfortable position of interviewing the program director's son for admission to Dartmouth. When the program director, who was much higher than me on the Lockheed Martin corporate ladder, came to my cubicle to discuss his son's candidacy, I felt like there was a little bit of an edge to his tone. Dartmouth enlists alumnus volunteers across the country to interview high school students seeking admission to the college, and I happened to be one of those volunteers in the Denver area. I did my best to paint his son's candidacy in a positive light, but ultimately his son was not admitted to the college. Shortly after that, I was moved to a different rotation.

While working with the IT department, it was fascinating to learn some of the cybersecurity challenges a company like Lockheed faces when trying to protect national secrets. At the time the company was struggling with Chinese hackers that were trying to hack the Space Systems network on a daily basis. Lockheed employed its own hackers, but these hackers would not acknowledge their employment with Lockheed in order to save face in the hacker community. They would go to all the hacker conferences and stay on top of the latest techniques, and then report back to the company regarding cybersecurity threats on the horizon. I also learned why one of the military complexes in our Denver plant didn't have any windows. It turns out that windows pose a security threat other than the obvious visual one. I learned about spy technology where someone could point a sensor at a window, and through the vibrations of the window, they could capture computer keyboard keystroke sounds and convert those vibrations into text with an alarmingly high accuracy. This way a spy could capture the login credentials of an employee with a top-secret clearance and open up the entire server to bad actors.

The Orion program is an ongoing effort to replace the outdated Space Shuttle program and provide space transportation to the International Space Station, to the moon, and eventually to Mars as well. For one of my rotations, I worked as a thermal analyst on the proposal, before Lockheed was awarded the contract in competition with other aerospace juggernauts. The proposal work was intense and included some of the most challenging problems I've encountered in my entire career. At the height of this intensity, I was deriving my own fourth-order differential equations to model radiative heat transfer to model the scenario when the Orion module is docked onto the International Space Station. My manager and I made several trips down to NASA's Johnson Space Center in Houston, TX, to make presentations to NASA personnel showcasing our work. Lockheed was awarded the contract, and I was able to do a rotation on the program as a structural analyst once the program was in house. In particular, I was focused on the interface between the crew module and the Launch Abort System.

The crowning achievement of my time at Lockheed Martin came with my final rotation in the Mission Operations department. It was there that I assumed the role of a mission controller, also sometimes referred to as an 'Ace'. Mission controllers take mission instructions generated by the systems engineers and relay them to assets in space via the Deep Space Network. While in mission operations, I communicated directly with the Mars rovers Spirit and Opportunity. Mission operations work sometimes required working the night shift to send out instructions at critical times. The highlight of my time in the Mission Operations department was when we landed the Phoenix Mars Lander on the surface of Mars. As highlighted previously, I worked on the development of the Phoenix Mars Lander as well, so being able to be a part of the mission operations team landing it on Mars was a special treat. Once we discovered that the lander had landed safely on Mars, one of the team leaders literally got up on his work desk and started dancing with joy, with not a care in the world for the mission-critical papers on his desk that he was inadvertently kicking in all directions. At no other time in my career have I experienced the excitement and sheer wonder that came when the Phoenix Mars Lander beamed back its first pictures of the Martian terrain. The governor of Colorado visited our mission operations area to join with us in celebrating the success of the program.

With all this excitement, and all of the cool programs I got to work on, why would anybody leave for a different company? There were really two driving factors that led to my departure from Lockheed Martin after my mission operations rotation. Firstly, the aerospace industry generally is very top heavy, which means opportunities for advancement are extremely limited. Even if you are one of the brightest engineers, you're still expected to put in many years as an engineer before they let you rise up the ranks, lead a team, or direct a program. I was extremely ambitious at the time and didn't have the patience to be an engineer for 10 to 15 years before becoming a leader in my field. Secondly, in spite of how exciting the programs are in space exploration, engineering compensation caps out quickly. Our family was continuing to grow, and even after achieving a promotion during my three years at the company, our family expenses were growing faster than my compensation was. After brainstorming all the solutions we could think of, we decided on a path that would lead to a better outcome, not only for my career ambitions, but also for my future compensation potential: business school. We moved our family from Denver, CO, to Lindon, UT, and I started full-time business school at BYU's Marriott School of Management in the late summer of 2008.

16

FLIRTING WITH ZÜRICH

We sold our home in Highlands Ranch, CO, and became renters again when we moved to Lindon, UT, for business school. We sold our house for about $25,000 more than we paid for it, but the equity from the proceeds of the sale were quickly swallowed up by various costs associated with the new business school adventure. We found a nice house to rent in the foothills of Mount Timpanogos in Utah. We settled in and I started business school. I left early in the morning, came home around dinner time, helped put the kids to bed, and then worked on homework and projects until around midnight. Then I would go to sleep and do it all over again the next day. What I didn't learn until later was that many of my classmates, even married ones, would hang out with each other throughout the evening. I chose to spend evenings with my family, but as a result, I ended up leaving business school without some of the strong relationships that my peers had formed.

Along the way I was hoping to find a subject that I was passionate about. Some of my peers had entered business school knowing exactly what they wanted to do afterwards. With my engineering background, I figured my skillset would be suited towards a job in finance, but I found it tremendously difficult to narrow down the possibilities will all the different finance jobs in the workplace. My first encounter with something that felt right was when a Swiss firm founded by a BYU alumnus came to campus for an info session. This firm was founded as one of the pioneers in private equity secondaries in Europe, and they gradually expanded their reach globally and entered other private investment asset classes as well. The words of the company's representative resonated strongly with me:

"We have a lot of business school students express interest in our firm. However, most of these students expect job openings to be simply delivered through the career center. Then when we go to check our inbound calls, we see that most of these students haven't even bothered to call us. If you want to stand out from the rest, you need to be bold in showing us how interested you are," he said.

What could be bolder than flying out to Switzerland and showing up at their headquarters unannounced, I wondered. We managed to find a babysitter so that Sarah could join me on the trip. We planned it so that we would fly to Zürich, Switzerland, I would meet with the private equity firm in Zug, then we would take a train to Budapest, Hungary, for my interview with Boston Consulting Group. We would then fly home from Budapest. After renting a car in Zürich, we drove out to Zug and I headed into the company's lobby. I approached the lady at the reception.

"I'm an MBA student from BYU in Utah in the United States. I don't have an appointment, but I flew out here to take a tour of your facilities, and I was wondering if any of your investment professionals would be willing to show me around," I inquired.

After her initial shock wore off that I would take such a risk, she replied, "Let me see if I can find someone."

After a few minutes of waiting, the founder's brother-in-law showed up and started showing me around the place. We discussed the various work areas of the company and what life was like in the Zürich area. After we spent some time together in discussion, I thanked him for the tour and departed.

Later that evening Sarah and I were having dinner in a small restaurant attached to our hotel. The native language in Zürich is Swiss German, which has a softer sound than German but was just as unintelligible to us. An older gentleman at the table next to us heard us speaking American English and introduced himself. It turns out he was from Colorado, where we had just moved from for business school, so we immediately found some common ground and had a great conversation.

"What brings you out here to the Zürich area?" I asked.

"I decided to start my own business while still living in Colorado. This little town of Zug has one of the lowest corporate tax rates in the world, so I decided to move out here and start the business here," he replied.

We found the residents of Zürich to be unusually cheerful and friendly, which made for a fun trip. After a quick trip to the museum in

Zürich, we finished our stay in Switzerland and caught our train to Budapest.

My visit to Hungary with Sarah was the first time I had been back to the country since my mission in the late 1990s. We rented a car, and I took her to see some of the sights around Budapest before I had my interview with Boston Consulting Group. The interviewer was a native Hungarian and welcomed me into the conference room. We engaged in some small talk in Hungarian before the main part of the interview started. The interviewer presented me with a case, which happened to be a company that specialized in pet food distribution in Europe. It was while I was working through that case that I realized I wanted nothing to do with the management consultant industry. I left the interview with a new sense of focus, crossing a major interest off my list of potential careers. We finished our stay in Budapest and headed back to the United States.

There was a popular job fair for MBA students taking place in New Orleans in 2009. The career services department at BYU was encouraging students to attend, and many of my business school classmates were planning on going. In addition to the prospect of securing an internship at the job fair, I had for years looked forward to an opportunity to visit New Orleans and enjoy the world-class music and food that city had to offer. As the date of the job fair inched closer, I decided it was time to book my travel and hotel for the event. I sat down at my desk at home and navigated to the job fair website on my laptop in order to register. As soon as I got to the job fair website, I felt a strong feeling warning me not to go. I didn't think much of it and moved on to work on something else. Several days later the topic of the job fair came up again while I was at the business school, and I decided again that I would register and book travel that evening. I came home and sat down in front of my laptop and navigated to the job fair website again. As I started typing information into the registration fields, that same warning feeling came to me again. Not wanting to ignore the spiritual prompting for a second time, I came to the conclusion that I wasn't supposed to attend that job fair. To this day I don't know what would have happened if I had ignored the prompting and gone anyways, but I am grateful for whatever protection or guidance that prompting provided me.

The need to secure a summer internship became a more pressing matter than determining what role I would prefer for full-time employment after business school. I ended up interviewing for a variety of corporate finance roles and secured an internship at American Express in New York. It didn't seem feasible for us to move the whole family to New York, since we had just had our sixth child in May 2009. We decided that I would sublet one of the New York University dorms just north of the Lower East Side of Manhattan for the summer, and I would fly back to visit the family every few weeks. I started taking the subway to and from work and walked by the 9/11 memorial site every day, which at the time was still a massive construction mess.

Just two weeks into my internship, I received an email from the brother-in-law of the founder of the private equity firm I had visited in Switzerland. An opening had become available in their Zug office where I would actually be working directly with him. The typical progression for MBA graduates from the United States was to rotate between the different business units at the Zug headquarters, and then return to the New York office for long-term employment. However, this opportunity would keep me there in Zug, Switzerland, permanently. There was an additional catch to the opportunity as well. Due to the time sensitive nature of filling the role, they needed me to not only quit my summer internship that I had just started, but also quit business school altogether and move out to Zug to start working. The compensation package was attractive. They offered 5 weeks of vacation, and Swiss culture was such that they expected you to take all 5 weeks off throughout the year. Additionally, as an incentive to improve the country's declining birth rate, the Swiss government at the time offered an additional stipend of 2,500 swiss francs per child per month, which with our family size would have been a very nice enhancement to the deal. It seemed like a tremendous opportunity and making the decision was very difficult, but in the end we decided to stay in the United States. Having such a large family in the Zürich area seemed unfeasible, and we also were concerned about living so far away from family in the States.

I completed my internship in New York and enjoyed the rest of my time in the big city. I frequented as many of the city's museums as I could discover, and the Metropolitan Museum of Art remains my favorite museum in the world. I also enjoyed hanging out at Union Square, as there was always a positive, vibrant energy to that place, and it was quite close to my summer residence. My only celebrity sighting over that summer was physically bumping into Noah Emmerich on the corner of an intersection on a rainy day in the Lower East Side. The amount of rainfall I experienced during the summer of 2009 in New York City was prodigious. After I commented on the excessive precipitation to a native New Yorker, he replied, "We actually sometimes get more rain than Seattle, but they're the ones that get stuck with the stigma." In spite of the wonderful time I had in New York over the summer, I realized that a family my size could not feasibly live in Manhattan, and I was not a fan of having a longer commute, so I decided against pursuing any of the many financial job opportunities in the New York City area.

I returned to Utah from my internship with a renewed focus on discovering my passion. I could tell from my first-year accounting class and my summer internship that accounting and corporate finance were not going to keep my attention. However, in my second year of coursework, I took classes in investments and derivatives, and I almost immediately felt a strong spark of passion in both subjects. I had discovered what I was interested in, and it only remained to find a job opportunity in the general area of investment management.

A couple professors and a group of us MBA students took a trip to Europe to explore additional opportunities in that part of the world. Our trip included stays in London, Geneva, Vevey, and Zürich. In London we visited the National Gallery and Chinatown during some downtime we had. We had meetings at Barclays headquarters and the Credit Suisse office in London. In Vevey we visited Nestlé headquarters and learned about corporate finance opportunities with their firm. In Zürich we visited Credit Suisse headquarters for some meetings in the private wealth management space. We also visited the private equity firm in Zug where I had already declined an offer. The highlight of the trip came when we were in a conference room on one of the upper floors of the Credit Suisse building in London. After we were all seated, a high-level Credit Suisse executive entered the room and started greeting each of us individually. He started sharing some general business advice about how he rose to his current position. One piece of wisdom he shared was the following:

"I have been in plenty of situations where I knew I wasn't the smartest guy in the room. However, I've always been the hardest working guy in the room, and that's how I got to where I am today."

He also shared a unique job opportunity with us. "I have an investment banking position open in Dubai, and I'm happy to give the job to one of you. However, if you're interested, I need to know that you really want this, and that you will work your tail off in that office," he announced.

Upon returning to the States, I decided to look into the Credit Suisse investment banking job in Dubai. I found an American investment banking associate there, and we scheduled a call that worked for both of our time zones.

"It's a death machine here," he said. "I feel like I'm dying. I'm sure my job prospects will be excellent if I ever leave this place, but I'm not enjoying this."

This wasn't my first conversation with a current or former investment banker, but the way he described it definitely set off some red flags in my mind. I valued my roles as a husband and father, and I also valued a decent night of sleep. The long hours of investment bankers would materially diminish the amount of time I would have with my family. My conversation with him ended up convincing me to not pursue investment banking opportunities any further.

I started interviewing for private wealth management jobs in the Los Angeles area and started getting some traction in the space. I made it to the final round of interviews at both Barclays and Goldman Sachs. At the time Barclays had a requirement that a candidate would not be hired unless every interviewer was in favor of hiring that person. I had a 'mole' at Barclays who told me what went on behind the scenes. He said that every interviewer there except one was a 'yes' on my candidacy. When the other members of the team pressed the one guy on why he was a 'no' on my candidacy, he responded, "He doesn't have the look." Private wealth management roles have a very heavy sales component, and everybody knows that having good looks can be an important part of that kind of job. One of the most notable interview questions I received at Barclays was when one of the interviewers held up my resume and asked me:

"What do you think are your most impressive accomplishments on your resume?"

I responded with a few highlights that I thought were exceptional.

"Wrong," he responded. "The fact that you landed a spacecraft on Mars, and that you sold religion for two years in a foreign country and in a foreign language are the most impressive accomplishments listed here."

His tone was so condescending that in that moment I couldn't tell whether I should beam with pride regarding those achievements, or hang my head in shame for answering the question incorrectly from his perspective. In the end it didn't matter, as that same interviewer was the one that didn't care for my physical looks.

The interviews at Goldman also led to a dead end. The most peculiar interview at Goldman was one in which a gentleman came into the room where I was already seated and proceeded to just stare at me for several minutes without saying a word. When the next interviewer came into the room, I couldn't help but ask what the previous guy was doing.

"Oh, that guy? Yeah, he does this thing where he feels like if he stares at someone long enough, he thinks he can sense what aura they're emitting. Most of us think it's nonsense, but he's one of the senior members of the team and stands by his methods," she replied.

Rather than press on in the private wealth management space, I decided to redirect my efforts towards more of an investment analyst role, where they would care more about my skillset rather than my physical appearance.

As luck would have it, a small insurance company with about $3 billion in assets in Salt Lake City was looking for a corporate bond analyst. I interviewed with various members of the team before sitting down with the Chief Investment Officer. He had started his career in investment banking at Solomon Brothers back in the 1980s and had then moved over to Deutsche Bank, rising to a global head position in structured credit. In the middle of our conversation, he abruptly took the discussion in a different direction.

"I used to hire former engineers all the time when I was doing structured credit at Deutsche Bank. The engineering skillset seemed to fit well with structured credit, and many former engineers became some of our best structured analysts. With this job posting, we were really looking for someone to be a corporate bond analyst. However, I think you'd be a better fit in structured credit if that's something that would interest you," he said.

I felt that he was in a better position than I was to know where I would excel. Without knowing much of anything about structured credit, I took his advice and took a position as a structured credit analyst on his team, starting full-time after the completion of business school. We moved the family up to Salt Lake to be closer to the job. The home we were renting was in Cottonwood Heights and was less than 30 minutes from some of the best snow skiing on earth, but with no skiers in our household, this benefit was lost on us. I actually took a pay cut from what I was making as a promoted, leadership-track engineer at Lockheed Martin before entering business school. However, I now had my foot in the door in a much more lucrative industry, and I was willing to take the gamble that my compensation would soon outpace what I could ever have hoped to obtain in the engineering industry. This gamble eventually paid off within a few years' time. While the work I now do is arguably less meaningful than the exciting programs I worked on at Lockheed Martin, I am now in a better position to provide for our large family, and I enjoy the financial work I do.

Around the time I finished business school, my sister graduated with her bachelor's degree from Northern Arizona University in Flagstaff, AZ. It wasn't feasible for us to bring down the entire family for the event, but I definitely wanted to attend her graduation ceremony and share that special experience with her. I hopped in our red 1998 Ford Escort and started driving down from Utah to Flagstaff, AZ. About half an hour south of Provo, UT, lies a small town by the name of Santaquin with a population under 15,000 as of the 2020 census. I was in good spirits, had my music playing in the car, and was enjoying the trip so far as I entered the Santaquin area. All of a sudden, I started feeling a very dark presence, and I slowly reached over to my phone and turned off the music. I started paying closer attention to what I was feeling, and I sensed that the dark presence was aware of me. That awareness quickly morphed into a deep, burning hatred directed towards me, and I could tell that the presence wished intense physical harm upon me. I have never in my life felt anything as sinister as I felt during those moments. As if the veil had been parted in order for me to feel that and have that experience, the dark presence slowly dissipated moments later. We know from the Book of Revelation in the New Testament, chapter

12, verse 9, that "the great dragon was cast out, that old serpent, called the Devil, and Satan, which deceiveth the whole world: he was cast out into the earth, and his angels were cast out with him." Regarding the angels that were cast out along with Satan, we also know that their work is to tempt mankind. I've always thought of them as dispassionate accountants working for the wrong team, but this powerful spiritual experience quickly changed my thinking.

17

FATHER OF NINE

To preface this chapter, let me just say that my family is by far the most important thing in my life. I cherish my wife and children and derive more satisfaction from them than any dream job or passion hobby could ever provide. One of my advanced readers asked, "If family is so important to you, why do you only dedicate two chapters to being a husband and father?" My response to that is that this book is not intended to be a chronicle of what has been most important to me in life. If that were the intent, then the vast majority of the book would be related to family and spirituality. I may write that book someday, but this book is not that.

Getting married at a young age, and even having children at a young age, can be quite common in some geographical parts of the country or among certain religious or cultural demographics. However, doing both while still an undergraduate at an Ivy League institution is extremely rare, and Sarah and I fell into this category. I was 22 and she was 19 at the time of our marriage in November 2000. Sarah had our first child, Micaela, in January 2002, when we were both still undergraduate students. We had plenty of people think we were crazy for getting married so young, and this sentiment only strengthened once we started bringing a baby in a baby carrier to the college cafeteria.

When Sarah first became pregnant with Micaela, she went to the student clinic to complete a formal pregnancy test. Once the results were in, the nurse walked into the room and nonchalantly said, "Your pregnancy test was positive. We can schedule you for Tuesday or Thursday." When Sarah looked confused, the nurse added, "Those are the only days we perform terminations." To their surprise, Sarah made it clear that she had no intention of having an abortion and that we were happy to welcome this child into our family.

In spite of starting marriage and family so early, and contrary to the expectations of both students and faculty that were in our circles of influence, Sarah and I continued to excel in our studies. Sarah finished Dartmouth in three years and graduated with honors. I got my best grades after we got married, while my friends thought the exact opposite would be true. Ambitious Ivy League undergraduates thought of marriage and family as a distraction and limitation at such a young age. They saw it as an obstacle to pursuing their career-related dreams. Starting our family so early did end up delaying Sarah's career aspirations. However, she is now making up for lost career time with her medical school and residency journey. By starting so young, she got to spend a lot of time at home with our children while they were young and still has an illustrious medical career to look forward to in her near future.

Our oldest daughter Miceala was born in the dead of winter in New Hampshire. As we were preparing to leave the hospital as first-time parents, the snow was piled waist-high and there was a biting chill in the air. We bundled our tiny newborn in fleece and strapped her into the car seat. It was in that moment as I looked down at her in that carrier car seat that I felt my first wave of parenting panic. We had to take this little human home with us and care for her on our own, and I knew my life would never be the same. The moment of panic quickly passed and Sarah, Micaela, and I left the hospital as a new family of three.

While Sarah was pregnant with Micaela, I spent 8 weeks in the Dartmouth wood shop, primarily on the weekends, building a wooden cradle for Micaela. She slept in that homemade cradle until she outgrew it, which didn't take very long. She was a big baby with a healthy startle reflex, and she would fling her arms out to her sides after any unexpected noise. Her chubby little baby hands would smack the side bars of the cradle, not so much that it would cause her to cry, but hard enough that we could hear it from a different room – and we quickly realized she would be more comfortable in a larger crib.

We moved from our little rented house in Norwich, VT, into the graduate/married/family student housing in Hanover, NH, just down the road from the college. Sarah had technically completed her undergraduate coursework in 2001, but we decided to graduate together in June 2002. Micaela was 5 months old at the time, and Sarah decided to make a baby-sized graduation gown that Micaela could wear to commencement, so that she could match her parents. The college photographer saw the three of us together and decided to snap a quick picture on the main quad of the campus. Later after reviewing all the pictures he had taken during graduation, he liked ours enough that he decided to make it the cover of the graduation video. Anybody that bought a graduation video that year had a giant picture of Sarah, Micaela, and me on the cover.

After graduating from college I continued my graduate engineering studies, and in May of the following year, we welcomed our second daughter, Elizabeth, into our family. The following month I completed the requirements for my second bachelor's degree and my first master's degree. Micaela was a sweet older sibling to her new sister, and they both seemed to be happy and healthy. It was with Elizabeth (or Lizzie) that I learned an important lesson about changing diapers. One day as I started to change her poopy diaper, she suddenly reached down, took a firm hold of the poopy diaper that I had moved to the side, and quickly did a couple whip-like motions with her arm, sending poop flying everywhere. That was the day I learned the hard way that you always move the messy diaper out of reach of the baby you are changing. Lizzie moved quickly in other ways as well, as she started walking and talking at the young age of ten months old, which ended up being months earlier than the rest of her siblings.

I continued my graduate studies in pursuit of a second master's degree, and in August of 2004 we welcomed our third daughter, Rachel, into the family. While Sarah was in labor with Rachel, we both decided that I should go send a quick update to family on how it was going. At the time, I didn't have a smartphone that I could send a quick update from within the labor room. I had to exit the room we were in, go down a couple floors, and use a public computer terminal there to send a quick email to family and close friends. However, for some reason, I was taking my sweet time walking to and from that public terminal. I felt a sense of freedom from the stresses of the room in which Sarah was actively in labor. Once I casually arrived back at the labor room, I quickly noticed the room was full of healthcare professionals in full protective suits, and one of the professionals was literally using a hand to keep Rachel in the womb, as the baby was fully ready to exit. Sarah was worried that she was going to have the baby while I was gone checking my email. My feelings of casual freedom I had in the hall quickly turned into panic as I realized I had made a mistake in wandering about for so long. I could see clearly in Sarah's face that she wasn't happy with me either. In the end I was lucky to be present for Rachel's birth and learned a lesson about timing my activities while my wife was in labor!

The doctor that was tending to Sarah recommended that due to a complication with Rachel's birth that we should strongly consider not having any more children. We obviously didn't follow that counsel, and that isolated complication never recurred. We had outgrown the graduate housing that we were living in, and Sarah also thought it would be a good investment to buy a local condominium that was being offered cheaply. She ended up being right, and we made over $40,000 in less than six months after buying the condominium and making a number of upgrades. I finished my graduate work in November 2004 and took a job with a local engineering think tank until I received an offer to work with Lockheed Martin.

We lived in Denver for three years and welcomed two more children into our young family during that time. I originally thought that it would be nice to have at least two boys and two girls. However, after having three girls in a row, I started to wonder if we would ever have any boys. Our time in Denver proved that wrong, as we then had two boys in a row, first Andrew in March of 2006, and then William in September of 2007. Our family was growing quickly, and we made sure to buy a place with enough room for our new family additions. Sarah's wise condominium investment enabled us to have enough money for a down payment on a modest home in the Highlands Ranch area of Denver. Andrew and William are now both teenagers at the time of writing this book. Andrew has developed a love of making electronic music using FL Studio. He cites the experience of making electronic music with me when he was a young child using Reason and GarageBand as being inspirational for him. William is now taller than I am, coming in at 6'3" – even though he's only in eighth grade – and enjoys video games, hanging out with friends, and even cooking for the family on occasion.

As a young and sometimes immature father, I sometimes struggled with poor parenting habits. I would tend to view the toddlers and their childish behaviors as a burden and an obstacle to things I wanted to do with my life, rather than cherishing my time with them. I was also prone to raising my voice in anger at them when they disobeyed. Sometimes in my temper I would be very negative as I took them to their rooms, or some other timeout. Sarah was patient with me over the years, but always advocated for a gentler approach to parenting, focusing on teaching rather than punishing. In my heart I knew she was right, and I struggled for years to grow into the type of father I should be. It is a big regret to me now that I expressed so much anger and negativity to my older children when they were younger. I hope that I have been a better parent to my younger children and will continue to grow as a father, and hopefully grandfather, throughout my life.

Once we had five children, we started noticing certain commonplace activities becoming less manageable. The concept of flying somewhere with the entire family was cost-prohibitive, as well as mentally daunting as our five kids were ages five and under. Local family outings were also somewhat of a circus. Sarah and I looked for ways to provide fun experiences for the kids without leaving far from home, and we almost never got away together without the children. If I had to do it all over again, I think I would have tried harder to find ways for Sarah and me to make ourselves take occasional breaks from the kids for our own sanity, and just to re-energize. Instead, we both became work horses, as I focused on my career, and Sarah focused on her much more difficult job of being a stay-at-home mother and homeschool teacher to a growing number of children.

In spite of how busy the children kept her, Sarah found a way to start her own photography business. Specifically, she had invested in a very nice digital camera, associated lenses and flashes, and a number of backdrops. She had also honed her photography skills over the years with the portrait photography she had done of our own children and for friends and family. Word of her new company spread to a local moms' group, and her clientele grew rapidly and even expanded briefly into corporate photography. She enjoyed focusing on individual and family portraits in her in-home studio, and then she would offer post-photoshoot editing to get the pictures looking just right. Through trial and error, and depending on the pickiness of the client, she discovered that the photo editing portion of her job took more time and was less enjoyable than taking the pictures in the studio. Ultimately, her client base grew beyond what Sarah preferred, and she closed down the business to focus on taking portraits for friends and family.

In July 2008 we moved to Utah so that I could start business school at BYU. Around the same time, we decided to purchase a full-size van, a white Chevrolet Express 3500 with tinted windows, in order to accommodate our growing family. In May 2009, right before leaving for my MBA summer internship, we had our third boy in a row, Joseph. His birth was traumatic, as the umbilical cord was too short. As the short cord stretched during the birth, his oxygen levels dipped down dramatically, and the code alert started sounding in the room. A team of doctors and nurses rushed in, and he had to be revived after the birth. The whole ordeal was very scary, but luckily Joseph was fine, and the healthcare professionals there were excellent and prompt in handling the situation.

The first place we lived in during the business school experience was a nice-looking neighborhood near the foothills of the towering Wasatch mountain range, where the homes were nicer but the people frequently considered themselves literally and figuratively above others. We had a very tough time integrating into that community. It seemed none of our neighbors liked us or our children. Some of them wouldn't let their kids play with our children. Others were quite blatant about their dislike of our family. On one occasion, as Sarah was walking by the neighbor's house, his boy starting throwing snowballs at her. Instead of telling his boy to cut it out, the boy's father said nothing and instead just smiled. Another time, a neighborhood child told us, "My mom says your family's yucky." It seemed that the person that was nicest to us in that area was our kind Muslim landlord. One time when he stopped by to ask us how things were going, I asked him what had originally drawn him to move into a neighborhood that was 98% LDS. "We liked the thought of being surrounded by families with high moral standards in a low-crime area, even if they don't share our spiritual beliefs," he responded. He was right about those standards of behavior upheld by our neighbors. However, it seemed our family just didn't fit the mold well enough to be welcomed into this particular enclave, especially since we later had much better experiences in other parts of Utah. We wondered if our Muslim landlord had a similar experience, causing him to leave the area and rent out his former home, but we never asked.

18

THE MERRILL BABY FARM

During my summer MBA internship with American Express in Manhattan, I befriended one of my fellow interns. He was Indian and during one of our group discussions he shared about being Brahmin and what that meant. He was a very friendly, charming guy, and always seemed to have a smile on his face. During one of our personal conversations, he asked how many kids I had. When I told him we just had our sixth child before I started the internship, he all of a sudden got a very serious look on his face. He gently reached out his hand and placed it on my belly and left it there, and while maintaining eye contact, he said, "You are a very wealthy man." The act of him placing his hand on my larger-than-average dad gut was a bit awkward, but I could tell from his words and facial expression that he considered having so many children to be a blessing.

Once we had six children, while I was still in business school, I noticed people started treating me differently. Occasionally I wouldn't get invited to activities where the rest of what I thought were my friends would be doing something together. Later I would ask them why they didn't invite me, and they would just say some variation of, "Well, we thought you'd be too busy, considering how many kids you have." This type of exclusion was emotionally painful for me. However, rather than trying to fight the reputation of being too busy to hang out with friends, I just decided to embrace it and spend all my time with family. I enjoyed my classwork and discovered a strong interest in the investment side of finance.

After business school graduation, our family moved to the Salt Lake Valley as I started my career in finance. During the three years that we remained in Utah after business school, we had two more children. The first of those was our youngest daughter, Emma, in December 2010. The second was our fourth boy, John, in July 2012. Once we had 8 children, I started to feel like I was close to my limit as a father. Most parents reach this point well before their 8th child; perhaps I was able to make it to that point because Sarah was shouldering most of the burden. The second thing I noticed was that with 8 children, we were becoming more of a noticeable outlier even within the LDS church, which is known for having large families.

Emma has been full of happy surprises for us over the years. At a very young age we took note that she had somehow developed perfect pitch, the origins of which remain a mystery to us to this day. She has also on countless occasions demonstrated a strong eidetic memory, recalling events that happened long ago in unusually great detail. When mentioning a trip to a movie theater from years ago, she would remember what day of the week it was, what each person was wearing and where they sat, what theater number we were in, and so forth. I have never had a memory approaching that level of strength, so her abilities in this area have been quite astonishing to me. At the time of writing this book, she is still in elementary school but is excelling in her classes.

While still in Utah, we were involved in a car crash on a major highway in the Salt Lake area. We were headed south for Andrew's birthday party on I-15. I've driven highways in many different states, but the portion of I-15 in the Salt Lake area has one of the biggest problems I've seen with objects in the road. I've seen mattresses, couches, wooden pallets, garbage cans, furniture, and all sorts of other objects strewn across highway lanes. These obstacles obviously and quickly cause traffic accidents, and the police in the area are aware of the problem. The problem is not the fault of those responsible for cleaning up such messes, as the police would always address it and remove the debris promptly once they were notified. Rather the main problem was that there were so many people living in that area that would throw things in the back of their pickup truck or trailer without tying it down. In our particular case, there were a number of cubic metal crates strewn across a couple lanes, and the sedan in the lane just to our left swerved away from us in order to avoid the crates. However, the act of swerving at a high speed caused him to lose control of the vehicle, which subsequently drifted into our lane. I wasn't able to slow down the van soon enough, and the front left corner of our van slammed into the right side of the smaller sedan. Because the van was so much heavier than the little sedan, we felt a slight bump and crunch, but the jolt to us inside the van was not severe. However, the impact sent the little sedan spinning wildly away from the van. After the police came to address the accident, we discovered that the sedan had a young father and his small daughter in the car, and luckily both of them were fine. We had to have the van towed to a service shop to get repaired, and insurance covered it all fortunately. However, upon getting our temporary loaner vehicle, determined to not let the crash ruin our day, we continued our journey to the place of Andrew's party and had a wonderful birthday party with him and the rest of the family.

In spite of being surrounded by so many people of our same faith and also having so many members of Sarah's family live nearby, the dynamics of our family complicated our participation in some activities. Our children have never been the quiet, passive type. Understandably, a lot of people had difficulty handling the level of noise and movement that we had adjusted to over the years. Bringing that level of chaos into various public settings, and sometimes even just to family functions, could affect the ability of other participants to enjoy themselves. As a result of this, we started to naturally limit what activities we would do as an entire family, and instead would break off a small group of kids to join one or both parents for different activities. Sometimes our participation in extended family activities would also be limited by others that preferred not to experience our chaos on a regular basis. While I understand what must have been going through their minds, it was still painful for us to feel and experience that exclusion.

In 2013 I took an investment job in the Philadelphia area, and our ninth and final child, James, was born in February of the following year. Before James was born, our family scorecard was tied at four sons and four daughters, so the boys won the tie, and we occasionally refer to James as the 'tiebreaker baby'. We had been homeschooling the children until that time; however, once we moved to Pennsylvania, we were impressed with the quality of the schools in the Bucks County region, and Sarah and I felt the time was right to transition the children into public schools. The transition presented a few challenges, but nothing insurmountable, and the children were soon doing fine in their new public-school setting.

At my new job in Horsham, PA, I had a coworker who had five children. They started out having just one child. As they struggled to have additional children, they turned to in vitro fertilization (IVF) in order to increase their chances of conception. To their surprise, the IVF approach led to them having quadruplets, so they went from one child to five all at once. The quadruplets were approaching 10 years old, so the logistical issues of having quadruplet babies was behind them. However, he would still occasionally complain to the team about the struggles of having a large family. Once I joined the team, his complaining started decreasing, as he would glance over at me and realize whatever he was dealing with, I was dealing with twice as much – and if I wasn't complaining about it, then he probably shouldn't, either.

We have of course been on the receiving end of criticism and peoples' negative opinions over the years for having such a large family. Some have seen it as economically or ecologically irresponsible, considering the large amount of resources required to raise such a large family. Occasionally people would assume that because we had a large family that we must think everybody should do what we did, or that it's the 'best' or most ideal path for a family to take. The truth is that we believe the decision a couple makes in how many children to have is a very personal and even sacred decision. We have never judged anybody else for how many or how few children, if any, they have chosen to have. However, others have not always shown us that same level of open-mindedness. The most racist/classist reaction we received to how many kids we have came at a posh Dartmouth Club holiday party that Sarah and I attended in downtown Denver, CO, in the early 2000's. The party was full of wealthy white people, telling stories and arrogantly bragging about their accomplishments. In one group, when they found out how many children we had (5 at the time), one of the people in the group said, "Jason, you and Sarah having so many children is a wonderful thing. You're not the ones we're concerned about when it comes to overpopulation." I was saddened by the implication, as if educational or professional status conferred permission to have a larger family. We believe that children are a gift and sacred trust from God, and we felt incredibly grateful that He trusted us with so many members of His precious family. We also know very well that we are not inherently better than other families, and believe that all parents who honestly try to do their best for their families are living up to that privilege.

Sharing the fact that I have so many children has led to some very unexpected reactions from people over the years. During a work conference in Florida, I was seated next to a woman whom I had never met before. The topic of family came up, and I showed her the picture

260

of my large family. She let out a gasp in surprise, and then turned to me with a big smile on her face, grabbed my head with both her hands, and planted a massive, aggressive kiss on my cheek, right in front of all the other people at the dinner table, including my manager. "It's such a lovely thing that you have so many beautiful children!" she exclaimed. I've had similar experiences since then, where some women in particular find the large number of children I have to be a point of attraction, even though I'm a married man. I've even had others observe the behavior of these women from a third-party perspective, and the only way they've been able to describe it is as some sort of animal spirits attraction to virility.

One time during a professional conference in New York, I was attending a cocktail reception hosted by Goldman Sachs. At the event, my salesperson at Goldman introduced me as a Father of Nine to their head trader of commercial mortgage-backed securities (CMBS). The CMBS trader shook his head in disbelief, saying, "No way! I gotta see a picture of this." I pulled out my cell phone and showed him a picture of all eleven of us in our backyard in Doylestown, PA. After admiring the photo, he asked, "Would you be willing to text me that picture?" I thought the request seemed a bit odd, and he could tell I was reluctant by my reaction. "No, no," he replied, "It's not for anything weird. It's just that my wife and I just had our first child, and she's always complaining about how hard it is. So, the next time she complains, I'm going to show her this picture and tell her your story, so that she gains a little perspective!" I looked at him with a sly smile and told him, "Look, I know in your mind you think this is a good idea, but trust me, it's not. Every woman has her own limits and desires, and you gotta respect your wife's limits in this area and not try to turn her into someone else."

The approach we have taken to parenting has been very much the opposite of the popularized Asian Tiger Mother approach. We have sought to provide love and guidance along the way, and have encouraged productive and educational activities, but we've been very careful to try to not force the kids in any certain direction, such as requiring a particular sport or instrument. Rather we have pointed out to them that it's important for them to find what they're interested in and what they're passionate about and then perhaps pursue that, especially when it comes to future college studies and employment. We have coupled this approach with counsel about financial realities: if their passion leads them in a direction that doesn't pay very well, the financial stresses they may experience in life can quickly become overwhelming. I have seen both ends of that spectrum, where on the one side you have super wealthy people that are not happy, and on the other end you have very poor people that have spent their entire lives doing what they love and finding happiness and satisfaction along the way. We also teach the kids that if they're lucky, they'll find something that they not only enjoy, but that also pays well. Our approach with our children has thankfully led us to a point where we can see that the kids are for the most part intelligent, hard-working, and internally-motivated.

We have moved our family between states multiple times over the years, and some of our kids have cited these moves as being formative for them in various ways. Many parents try to move as little as possible while raising their kids, out of fear that uprooting the children can lead to long-term negative consequences. Our various moves have of course come at an emotional cost, especially for the older kids, but it has also helped teach our kids adaptability, flexibility, and that new relationships can add to, instead of replace, old ones. During one move across the country, one of our children said that moving had taught him that friendships are not always permanent, but that family is. Our kids were fortunate in that sense to have several friends and permanent playmates built into their home life, but we still felt sad for our kids and their friends with each move. We have tried to teach them how to keep in touch with loved ones in other states over the years, as they collected valuable experiences and lessons in each new home.

The true hero in the story of our family has of course been my extraordinary wife, who of her own free will carried, gave birth to, and subsequently raised so many children, all while delaying her career ambitions. I will never be able to match the sacrifice she has made to build such a beautiful family, and I owe all my happiness in life to her. Her adventurous spirit definitely played a part in her willingness to have such a large family, and to take all the ups and downs that come along with such a courageous endeavor. As our number of children grew, we would sometimes joke that we were running a farm, and we would sometimes laughingly refer to ourselves as the Merrill Baby Farm. Sarah has outworked me every year of our marriage, with all she has done to care for our children and myself. Along the way she has taught me to be a better husband, father, and man in general. Being a father to our amazing children has brought me immense joy and sense of purpose in life's journey, and it never would have been possible without her.

19

CRANBERRY AND SPRITE

When I worked at Lockheed Martin, telling people what I did for my job was a pleasure. I was a mechanical engineer working on a variety of exciting space exploration programs. Even though the job itself was incredibly complex, explaining what I actually did for my job to other people was pretty simple. People were always interested to hear about what type of space exploration I was supporting. Now that I'm in finance, it's almost as if the complete opposite is true. It is incredibly difficult to explain to finance outsiders what I do, and I can see other people's eyes glazing over out of boredom when I'm explaining my work. My job in finance is definitely less complex but more abstract than what I was doing in space exploration. That being said, I still enjoy it much more than my previous engineering career, and it most definitely pays the bills better. I would have much rather not written this chapter, as it is not my intent to bore the reader to death, and I've never considered my job to be a thing that defines me as a person. However, some people do consider their career to be a defining characteristic of who they are, and so that's what they may want to know or learn about when they're getting to know somebody else. Additionally, putting it all down on the page this way can perhaps reduce the number of repeated questions I get, even from family members, regarding, "What is it exactly that you do again?"

I'm going to use some examples to illustrate what the two main types of investors are. You have a millionaire friend in your neighborhood who gives his 12-year-old son $5,000 and lets him use his trading account to start playing the stock market. An uncle of yours who has no training or education in investing starts buying some cryptocurrency. Your grandmother came up with a good stock pick at one point and now thinks she's a good investor. You retire and hire a broker at a personal brokerage firm to manage your $2 million in retirement money. These are all examples of 'retail investors', where smaller amounts of money are involved, and the typical investments being bought and sold are considered to be less complex. On the other end of the spectrum, institutional investors deal in much larger quantities and much more complex financial assets. Institutional investors include banks, hedge funds, insurance companies, and institutional money managers, among others. At these types of institutions, there is typically just a very large pile of money to invest resulting from either the overall operations of the company or investments from external institutional clients. My job is on the institutional investor side at an insurance company. I manage over $2 billion in fixed income securities (i.e., bonds), and my company has over $30 billion in assets under management. The bonds I buy and sell are called collateralized loan obligations (CLO), and there are Qualified Institutional Buyer (QIB) restrictions that make it impossible for a retail investor to directly buy CLO securities. The existence of these QIB restrictions is one type of evidence that institutional investors deal in more complex investments than retail investors do.

As an example of this complexity, let me describe what a CLO is. Let's say there's a hypothetical small company called Dumb

Workhorse Technologies, which we'll call DWT for short. DWT is rated single B by Moody's, which is a reputable rating agency. The single B rating signifies that DWT is a 'junk-rated' company, which suggests that DWT has a higher likelihood of going bankrupt compared to a higher-rated company. In spite of the low rating on the company, DWT is growing and is looking for capital to fund that growth. DWT approaches a bank and applies for a senior secured loan. Due to the size and revenue profile of DWT, the bank decides to broadly syndicate the loan, which means the loan is distributed across multiple loan investors, rather than the bank keeping the entire loan on its own books. Some of these loan investors just keep their portion of the loan on their own books as an investment. However, the biggest loan investor type is known as a CLO manager. These CLO managers buy a bunch of loans like this, and once they reach a critical mass of loans on their balance sheet, typically around $500 million or so worth of loans, they then repackage those loans into a new investment vehicle called a CLO. The CLO manager finds an investment bank to help issue the CLO and syndicate (distribute and sell) it to CLO investors. Once the CLO is issued, the CLO issuer gets the net present value of future principal and interest cash flows from the underlying loans, minus various deal fees charged by the investment bank. The CLO investors are then entitled to the actual future principal and interest cash flows from the underlying loans. The CLO is also divided into different tranches that have different ratings, different levels of risk, and different interest rates. I have been an investor in CLO and other exotic fixed income securities on behalf of a handful of insurance companies over the past 12 years since I graduated from business school. I have been recruited by a couple of high-profile hedge funds during this time as well, where I would have worked longer hours and made much more money. However, I ended up declining those opportunities and staying on the insurance side of the business in order to maintain a better work/life balance.

I don't consider my work to be very noble. When I was involved in space exploration at Lockheed Martin, that seemed like something more meaningful and interesting to the public. Now what I do just seems to make rich corporations get richer. Corporations in a capitalist society seem to be one of the modern-day allocators of capital among the working class through the wages they pay to employees. A quick look at wage growth over the past 100 years shows that corporations have definitely become richer while the purchasing power of employees has definitely not increased in a similar fashion. This low wage issue is one of the reasons why so many Americans feel that they're constantly working so hard but never able to get ahead.

As I write these memoirs, I am currently still in this industry, so it's important that I keep names of certain people, companies, and information confidential. This is important in order to protect the reputations of myself and those people and companies that I have worked with over the years. However, I will do my best to share some stories that are entertaining and informative with respect to the finance career I have enjoyed over the past several years.

One of the stark differences between the engineers I worked with at Lockheed Martin and the Wall Street professionals I deal with on a daily basis is with regards to what the people are like. At Lockheed Martin, the people I worked with were generally very intelligent, but lacking in ambition and social skills. God, family, and country tended to be things that were more important than the job to a lot of these folks. Promotions were few and far between, but turnover at the company was very low. My entry-level salary at Lockheed was $65,000 per year, and this had increased to around $90,000 per year before I left for business school. However, it was not uncommon for even senior engineers that had worked at the company for decades to have their salary top out around $110,000 per year. If a young, ambitious engineer (which I was) wanted to move up the ladder, lead a team, or lead a program, you had to put in your dues and work at the company for at least 15-20 years before leaders at the company would let that happen. This culture was a true ambition killer for young, talented, motivated engineers. The idea of leaving engineering to go do something else was also very unusual in the company.

This culture and compensation structure is in contrast with what's found in the institutional investor industry. People in my corner of finance tend to be extremely hard-working, ambitious, highly energetic, and incentive-oriented. These characteristics tend to make up for the slight edge in intelligence that the rocket scientists have over the finance industry. However, the people in my corner of the finance industry tend to focus almost too much on their careers, even at the expense of family and personal well-being. They let their job define who they are in some cases. I currently work with over 40 broker dealers on

Wall Street with the trading I do, and I have occasionally run into some bad apples. These are the few that are willing to take advantage of others to get ahead. The existence of these bad apples is what forces investors to stay sharp and know what they're doing. I focus on being as honest as I can be, while not being gullible or naïve, and not letting others take advantage of me or my company.

In spite of all the ups and downs of my job, I absolutely love what I do. I wake up every morning excited to continue building whatever I'm working on, and I truly treasure the journey. As I write these memoirs, I'm currently in the best role I've had in my entire career and very much enjoying it. I talk with a lot of people in the industry that always have something to complain about, whether it's their manager, their compensation, their level of authority, etc. In my current role I can truly say I have nothing to complain about, and for that I feel very blessed. I have had difficult managers in the past, and from that experience I know that working for someone like that even for a couple weeks can feel like an eternity. My heart goes out to people stuck in those situations, and I hope they find the courage and the opportunity to leave their current job and find something better.

In Ray Dalio's 'Principles', he states, "Society rewards those that give it what it wants. That is why how much money people have earned is a rough measure of how much they gave society what it wanted." His observation seems to highlight the wealth disparity that our capitalist society has created. While this wealth disparity is emotionally frustrating for such a large number of Americans, his comments ultimately do make sense to me. Think of all the highest-paying jobs out there in American society. Overpaid professional athletes? Society wants to be entertained by sports. Highly-paid brain surgeons? Wealthy people don't want a brain tumor to be the end of them. Investment managers? Corporations and wealthy individuals care enormously about preserving and growing their wealth. The only criticism I can think of regarding his comment is that when he uses the word 'society', he's actually referring to government entities and wealthy corporations and individuals, which are the main capital allocators of society. This is clearly evident in that society does not tend to reward those that give it only what poor people want. This principle suggests that if you want to make money, you need to be involved in an area that has some crossover with the major capital allocators of society.

Ultimately, in spite of all the numbers, data, and analysis that I'm typically buried in for my job, I'm really in a relationship business. The relationships I have with Wall Street professionals, security issuers, and other institutional investors in the space are invaluable to my ability to be effective in the industry. Even though I typically don't socialize the same way most people do in the industry, I still want to be in the flow as much as possible. That's why if there's a 'happy hour', even though I don't drink alcohol, I will go for the conversation and comradery. Being there with others is an important part of building and maintaining relationships. However, this can be a struggle when I go to the annual industry conference in Las Vegas. Most of the people that I have business relationships with are focused on gambling, drinking, and visiting strip clubs during their time in Vegas. I have been invited to strip clubs by numerous dealers and CLO managers, even though they know I'm LDS and that LDS people don't go to strip clubs.

At this annual Vegas conference, it is common for the dealers to get tables at various nightclubs and invite buy-side investors to join them. There's plenty of alcohol flowing at these events, but I tend to show up, as I like spending time with my dealer friends and enjoying the club music. On one such occasion, a dealer had a table at the Marquee nightclub in the Cosmopolitan resort. The music was loud, people were dancing, and everybody seemed to be having a good time. The cocktail waitress assigned to our table sidled up to me and asked, "Can I get you anything to drink?" My favorite drink for nightclub activities is a Sprite mixed with cranberry juice, and all my dealer friends know this to be my usual. At that moment, the music was quite loud when I leaned over to her and yelled "Cranberry and Sprite" loudly over the music. She nodded with a smile and left the table to handle my request. A few minutes later she came back with my order, and I eagerly started drinking, as all the loud talking and dancing had made my throat dry. The drink felt unusually sharp and pungent going down, until I realized that the waitress had added alcohol to it. I motioned her aside and asked, "I asked for a cranberry and Sprite. Why is there alcohol in this?" With a confused look on her face, she replied, "We're all adults here, so when you asked for a cranberry and Sprite, I just assumed that you wanted vodka with your cranberry." That drink ended a 15-year run for me of having absolutely no alcoholic beverages. The last time I had an alcoholic drink was at that Chinese restaurant in Hungary with the alcoholic fruit tea.

After that nightclub experience, some of my dealer friends will now take the drink from the waitress and take a quick sip of it themselves before giving it to me, just to make sure there's no alcohol in it. It has been eight years since that accidental drink of alcohol, and I haven't had any more unexpected (or anticipated) alcoholic beverages since.

The institutional investment management industry has made significant progress in becoming more racially diverse since the predominantly Caucasian heydays of the 1980's. However, the industry does still seem very male-dominated. There are plenty of women in the industry, but they have materially lower representation at the management and executive levels. Another problem that continues almost unabated in the industry is the bias that has nothing to do with race or gender. At one of the places I worked, if you didn't drink, golf, and gamble, you were never going to be in the inner circle and would be passed over when it came time for promotions. I'm told by friends across the industry that this behavior can be all too common. Many hiring managers, chief investment officers, or portfolio managers only want to hire people that look and act like they do. They want to look at their junior people and feel like they're looking in a mirror, I suppose. One of the biggest culprits of this kind of toxic behavior is hidden in the concept of 'cultural fit'. It's common for investment teams to consider 'cultural fit' when they're interviewing candidates. What does 'cultural fit' mean, though? Does someone need to communicate the same way the hiring manager does? Do they need to have the same style of dress, the same political beliefs, the same (lack of) religious beliefs? The same hobbies? If someone is very arrogant and has a large ego, and the rest of the team does not, then that could be a problem. Aside from that, I think that 'cultural fit' should be removed as one of the considerations in interviewing candidates. I remember a portfolio manager at a prior firm talking about an interview candidate, and he was ticking off a list of the candidate's positive characteristics to a group of other portfolio managers. One of the characteristics he listed was "he takes golf seriously." Really? That's one of your hiring criteria? Golf is just one of any number of hobbies that a person might have. Why would a successful candidate need to have the same hobby as the leaders on the team? This type of bias seems a bit ridiculous to me, in spite of how common it is. If you're one of those people that think, "Golf is more than just a game," I have news for you: that's how people feel about their non-golf hobbies as well.

When hiring junior people, my corner of the finance industry tends to attract top talent at universities across the country, due to the outstanding compensation and prestige compared to other industries. It is not uncommon for investment management firms to target 4.0 GPA type candidates out of undergraduate programs. I personally have had the opportunity to mentor and train a large number of these 4.0 GPA type junior employees. While doing this I have made some observations where the 'max intelligence' approach to hiring has actually failed us. It is true that what we do requires a minimum level of intellectual horsepower, or the person will not succeed in this competitive industry. However, there are some characteristics that I've noticed successful junior analysts possess that have less to do with raw intelligence.

The first characteristic is a willingness to figure out what needs to be done and do it, without needing to be spoon-fed projects and tasks. If you're a junior person and always asking senior folks on the team to give you something to do, they will perceive that as a burden. Another characteristic is attention to detail. I've noticed that some very smart junior analysts will be so focused on delivering results quickly that it will come at the sake of accuracy, and accuracy can be paramount in certain economic situations. A third characteristic is a willingness to build something new and create your own models, not just push the button on existing models. The fourth characteristic would be a willingness to wear a lot of hats. Some junior analysts come in thinking that their job will be very focused and fit into a tidy job description. That is rarely the case, and senior members of the team need the junior folks to be nimble, agile, and able to embrace change. They need them to be willing to take on ad hoc tasks and projects from time to time. Ultimately, we also need junior folks that understand what it means to be a professional, which means doing whatever it takes to get the job done. Don't play the victim and hide poor performance behind excuses. Take ownership of your mistakes, be honest about them, learn from them, and move forward.

20

BRAIN SURGERY SLEEPER CELL

The Urban Dictionary defines a sleeper cell as "A person who remains a dormant member of a group while belonging to another group for undisclosed reasons. Usually, the sleeper cell status is kept a secret."

From the time we discovered that we were expecting our first child in the Spring of 2001, Sarah started a phase where she was either pregnant or nursing while being a stay-at-home mom for the majority of the next 15 years. Over the years while she was changing literally thousands of diapers, she kept her career dreams alive, and would take classes and work in academic research as time and circumstances allowed. She and I would occasionally talk about what she would have done if she hadn't gone down the path she was on, and we both knew she was meant to pursue professional ambitions at some point. Sarah graduated from Dartmouth with honors after only three years, and her intent was to go directly into medical school after completing her undergraduate studies. A few weeks after signing up for the MCAT, we discovered she was expecting our first baby. Although she went on to take that exam while five months pregnant, we began to feel that the direction of our lives was gradually changing.

I realize that some people consider being a stay-at-home mom a luxury of the wealthy. Some families, particularly single-parent families, may not have the option of having a parent stay home with the children. I am sensitive to that struggle, particularly since I grew up in a single-parent family myself, as did Sarah. In the early years of our own family, we struggled financially as well and counted every penny. However, the following discussion is largely addressing those that do have the option of stay-at-home motherhood.

Many women make the choice to be stay-at-home mothers, and that choice can sometimes be difficult or more complex for women who are particularly ambitious. The opportunity cost of time spent outside the professional realm can breed restlessness or even some dissatisfaction for many high-performing and intelligent stay-at-home moms. Although many mothers find ways to stay involved with their professional passions while home with their children, this balance doesn't lend itself equally well to all careers. For Sarah, it was a sacrifice to put her dream of medical school and a career as a physician on hold. However, I'm convinced that if Sarah had not chosen to devote some time as a stay-at-home mom, we definitely wouldn't have had our 9 beautiful children, and the children we did have would not have benefitted from the exceptional care they received from their mother.

As Sarah and I continued the conversation over the years, it was never fully clear to us how or when she would transition away from the stay-at-home mom life. After our youngest was born and we knew that our baby-having days were done, she began to feel the pull back to professional life more strongly. One evening while we were living in Doylestown, PA, she said, "I feel like it's time." After many conversations and some thoughtful prayer on the subject, we agreed that not only was it the right thing for her to do, but that it was also the right time. The sleeper cell was activated.

After being away from the academic realm for several years, there were some things Sarah had to do to prepare her medical school application. Medical students that apply more than a year after graduating from college are referred to as 'non-traditional', or 'non trad' for short. For such non trad students, post-baccalaureate science coursework, some clinical research, and retaking the MCAT exam are typical steps. She completed her post baccalaureate coursework at Harvard, her clinical research at University of Pennsylvania, volunteered as a Spanish medical interpreter at a local free clinic, and earned a competitive score upon retaking the MCAT. After applying to a small and carefully selected number of medical schools, she received offers of admission at the Mayo Clinic and Duke University, both of which are top-tier medical schools. After much consideration and internal debate, she decided to accept the offer of admission at the Mayo Clinic. Mayo has locations in Rochester, MN, Jacksonville, FL, and Scottsdale, AZ, and she chose the Scottsdale location.

Once the decision was made, the time came for me to notify my employer of our intentions. After one of our morning meetings in the

Spring of 2018, I asked my manager to stay behind with me in the conference room.

"There's no easy way to say this. Sarah got into the Mayo Medical School in Scottsdale, AZ, and I'm going to follow her out there," I told him.

"Is there a job on the other end?" he asked.

"No there is not," I replied. "If you need to let me go because of this, I understand. However, if you'd like to keep me on the team on a remote basis, I would love to continue working with you."

"Let me discuss with the leadership team and we will let you know," he responded.

A few hours later, he pulled me aside and shared the good news.

"We've decided were going to give this whole remote thing a shot," he shared.

We then gathered the rest of the team and made the announcement regarding my new remote work situation. As the news sank in with my coworkers, I returned to my desk and continued working. Slowly, some team members started coming over to discuss the move to get more details. My female coworkers seemed full of admiration for my wife that she was making such a move at that point in her life. My male coworkers had a much different take on it. Their comments ranged from "you're definitely a better husband than I am" to "I would never support my wife doing something like that."

We found a nice, large home to rent in Mesa, AZ, about 20 minutes from Sarah's new medical school, with 5 good-sized bedrooms and a wonderful pool for the kids. However, selling our existing home in Doylestown, PA, turned out to be a much more difficult task. Many potential buyers didn't like that the backyard was sloped or that they had to assume an 18-year contract for the installed solar panels. It didn't help that over the course of our 5 years in Pennsylvania, several new developments with brand-new homes had sprung up in our area, driving down the price of the older homes such as ours. We ended up having to do a short sale almost a year after moving out, and lost the $90,000 in equity that we had invested in the home.

Once in medical school, Sarah made the transition from stay-at-home mother to high-performing medical school student seamlessly. She not only excelled in her medical school coursework, but she also outperformed in her board exams, her research efforts, and networking with physicians and scientists. She logged countless hours in operating rooms across the country as she completed a wide variety of clinical rotations as part of her training. She also made many friends in her med school class and found time to enjoy those friendships, while remaining an outstanding wife and mother.

Due to her unique background, combined with her outstanding dedication and passion for neurosurgery, Sarah started to become more well-known on social media and in the neurosurgery industry. A variety of local news organizations, blogs, and podcasts reached out to her as media outlets became aware of her amazing story. As she is naturally more private and not a fan of the spotlight, she chose to turn down most of the initial media inquiries and instead maintained her focus on the journey towards medical residency.

As she started applying to different residency programs, she received a lot of interest and many interview offers from programs across the country, despite some discouragement she received from various people along the way. The prevailing wisdom at the time was that a student needed to get at least 15 interviews in order to maximize their chances at matching to a residency. Despite applying to a smaller-than-average number of residency programs, Sarah received well over the 'necessary' number of interviews and started feeling more confident in her ability to match to a neurosurgery residency.

After completing all of her interviews, the match process became a waiting game, with a focus on ranking programs. This period of ranking and waiting was fraught with anxiety, as the residency match process is truly one of those times in life where the applicant has very little control over where they end up living and training for multiple years. There was a tremendous amount of emotion, both good and bad, that went along with the process. These memoirs don't seem like the right venue to delve deeper into those emotions and experiences, so I will leave those to Sarah to expound upon in her own memoirs if she sees fit to do so.

Match day came and all the kids took the day off of school so that we could attend the matching ceremony in person. After a few speeches from the medical school administrators, the match envelopes were handed out and the attendees then mingled for a half hour before the designated match envelope opening time. Sarah had thought maybe we would stay in Arizona, but to her surprise she matched with the neurosurgery program at Indiana University! We're off to a new adventure this summer of 2022, as we once again move our large family across the country, this time headed to Indianapolis. The number of different states we have lived in continues to grow. After 7 years of residency in Indianapolis, Sarah will be eligible to work as a fully-trained brain surgeon. We have occasionally talked about how fun it would be if I were to return to rocket science once she is a practicing brain surgeon, just for the jokes.

THE END

www.ingramcontent.com/pod-product-compliance
Lightning Source LLC
Chambersburg PA
CBHW020436130626
46549CB00001B/169